PLAYBOOK FOR CHRISTIAN MANHOOD

12 KEY PLAYS FOR BLACK TEEN BOYS

JAMES C. PERKINS

Jean Alicia Elster, editor

Foreword by W. Wilson Goode, Sr.

JUDSON
PUBLISHERS
VALLEY FO

D0813365

Playbook for Christian Manhood: 12 Key Plays for Black Teen Boys
© 2008 by Judson Press, Valley Forge, PA 19482-0851
All rights reserved.

Bible quotations in this volume are from the New Revised Standard Version of the Bible, copyright © 1989 by the Division of Christian Education of the National Council of the Churches of Christ in the United States of America. Used by permission. All rights reserved.

Library of Congress Cataloging-in-Publication Data

Perkins, James C.
    Playbook for Christian manhood : 12 key plays for black teen boys / James C. Perkins, Jean Alicia Elster, editor.
    p. cm.
    ISBN-13: 978-0-8170-1525-1 (pbk. : alk. paper) 1. African American teenagers—Religious life. 2. Teenage boys—Religious life. I. Elster, Jean Alicia. II. Title.

    BR563.N4P45 2007
    248.8'3208996073—dc22

                               2007042259

Printed on recycled paper in the U.S.A.

First Printing, 2008.

To my grandson Chayton James Perkins
and the mighty men of the
Benjamin E. Mays Male Academy,
past, present, and future—

Gentlemen, these are the rules of the game.

Contents

Foreword

On any given day in America there are 1,542,244 African American males between 11–15 years of age. We know that many of them are at risk of not achieving their full potential. It is estimated that 56 percent of these young men are from single parent homes. For the most part, the majority of these males are not achieving as they should.

This is brought about by two issues. Many young African American males start first grade unable to compete with other students. They have had an insufficient learning environment at home, little or no pre-kindergarten, and inadequate kindergarten. Far too often these young boys enter first grade not ready to learn. The second challenge arises when these boys enter the sixth grade in an environment where learning and good conduct are not encouraged by their peers. In fact, in some schools and communities, being a good student is frowned upon. Unless young men are given the necessary tools to overcome these challenges, their grades slip, truancy persists, and behavior deteriorates. Eventually because of a combination of those factors, far too many young men drop out of school.

The future that might have held graduation, college, and a well-paid job, turns into life in the underground economy, where prison is inevitable. In fact, one in three of these young men will enter prison in their lifetime. And the process repeats itself over and over again. Children of incarcerated parents are the most likely to end up in prison themselves. I tell the story often about visiting a prison in Southeastern Pennsylvania and seeing a grandfather, father, and grandson in the same prison at the same time. While there the grandson wondered aloud to me whether he would see his son for the first time in prison.

In this powerful book, Dr. James Perkins outlines 12 plays for young African American teens that will set our young men on a clear path to success. Dr. Perkins has provided the necessary ingredients for young African American males to avoid poor school performance, behavioral difficulty, truancy, and eventual dropout. This book is the right prescription for the ills of African American males between the ages of 11 and 15. By using a football analogy, Dr. Perkins describes in clear and understandable terms how young African American males can avoid the pitfalls that trap so many. What is most impressive is that this book is not written by one who is advancing a theoretical concept, but by one with the experience of a true and tested model. Unlike so many, Dr. Perkins saw the problem more than 15 years ago and acted decisively. He started a school for boys in 1993 to teach these important lessons of life. These are lessons that propelled Dr. Perkins to success as pastor of a major congregation, school founder, and leader in national organizations. Not only have these lessons worked for Dr. Perkins, but they have worked for others.

The first plays in this book are the foundational ones: knowing who you are and knowing your passion. First, Dr. Perkins pointedly asks the question, "What do you want people to think of you when they hear your name?" This is a challenging and profound question that ought to provoke an inner self-assessment. How young men answer this question will determine their life chances. So often many of these young men spend their early lives surrounded by aimless, purposeless, and dreamless individuals who cannot see beyond their current circumstance. Dr. Benjamin Mays said, "It is not a calamity to die with dreams unfulfilled, but it is a calamity not to have dreamed at all. Not failure, but low aim is sin."

Dr. Perkins correctly points to education as a key play. What we have learned over the last decade is that education will, in many instances, ensure a person's successful outcome. Effective preschooling, all-day kindergarten, and excellent teachers of reading and math at the first-, second-, and third-grade levels can create on the part of African American males an appreciation for education. Effective mentoring programs with successful African American male role models can provide alternatives to what many young African Americans face daily in their environment.

But even if these things don't happen (and they won't in far too many instances), Dr. Perkins has prescribed the steps that could correct early failing in the sixth grade on. In the words of Dr. Perkins, "Another lesson I impress upon my boys is that when in class, they must listen to their teachers. The purpose of class is to get knowledge. The teacher is in charge of the classroom. And the teacher must be respected because the teacher has the knowledge that the student is there to get."

What Dr. Perkins has done with this play is put his finger on the simple most critical issue for any young teen. If the advice is heeded, success is all but guaranteed.

This is a book of wisdom for 11- to 15-year-old African American males. Naturally, it should be read by those young men themselves. In fact, school districts across the country should make this required reading for all male students between grades 6–9. The book is also essential reading for parents of those young men. Pastors, particularly youth pastors, should place this book on their must-read list. Mentoring organizations, especially those that mentor African American boys in this age range, should make this book a requirement for all mentors in their program as well.

Dr. Perkins has brilliantly woven real-life practical advice with proven research to present a roadmap for young African American males that should increase their likelihood of success. As such, he has made a major contribution to alleviating the negative factors that cause so many African Americans males not to succeed. Dr Perkins has scored a *touchdown* with this book!

Rev. Dr. W. Wilson Goode Sr.
National Director
Amachi

Kickoff:
Why This Book?

Basic Formation

I was sitting at my desk a while ago listening to a distinguished line-up of speakers pay tribute to the late Bo Schembechler, the legendary University of Michigan football coach. As a testimony to his 27 years as a college football coach—21 of those years at the University of Michigan—thousands of men filled the stadium to show their respects. They paid tribute to a man who had been a strong, lasting influence in their lives. Each speaker told some story about how "Coach Bo" had helped him to become a man. Each speaker emphasized some life lesson he learned from the trusted coach that molded his character and prepared him to build a future. You see, not only had he been their coach in *football*, he had also been their coach in *life*. He had been their life coach.

I want to do the same thing for you. I am writing this book—this manhood playbook—because I want to be *your* life coach.

Tackle

As an African American male, you are a precious commodity—a valuable resource that is increasingly rare. In fact, many people refer to you as an endangered species. This means that there is something happening in our American culture that is cutting down your odds of becoming an educated, successful, family man. Something sinister is happening in our society that is cutting down on your chances of being able to contribute to your community so that you can look back over the years and see a life well-lived.

As I write this playbook, I am assuming certain things about you. I am assuming that you are between the ages of 11 and 15. I am also assuming that you are roughly in grades 6 through 10. This means that you are at a critical point in your life where the decisions you make about yourself will pretty much determine what kind of future you will have.

Here's what the numbers tell us happens when young black males make the wrong decisions: While African American youth make up 14 percent of juveniles in the United States, they represent 40 percent of juveniles in prison. And the majority of these black youth are males! As you get older, the numbers do not look much better. These numbers also tell us that one-third of all black males will enter either a state or federal prison during their lifetime.

There is good news: Math and reading scores are going up for all students. Yet the scores for young black students, while improving, still lag far behind where they should be.

These numbers do not paint a bright picture about you and your future, do they? And folks would have you think that you might as well give up . . . that there's no hope. But remember— these are just numbers. And you, you are a living, breathing human being. You can think, plan, hope, and dream!

Running Play

And that is why I want to be your life coach. I want to give you the *12 key plays* that will help you *win in the game of life*. Master the lessons in this playbook, and you'll be on top of your game!

But why should you select me as your life coach? First, because I haven't done too badly using these lessons myself.

Now don't get me wrong—I am not, have never been, and do not ever expect to be perfect. But, the lessons I will share with you are the same ones I heard over and over from my father and other men I have admired over the course of my life. Because of the great respect I have for these men, I have tried these lessons and found them to be true. So, I want to be your life coach because I've tested and proven these lessons myself.

Passing Play

Next, I teach these 12 key plays to boys just like you every day. I started a school for boys in 1993 to teach them these same important lessons. I wanted to help them establish their lives on solid ground. I see these lessons taking root in them and changing their lives. I want to be your life coach because these lessons have not only worked for me, they are working for other boys just like you!

Goal Line

Finally, I want to be your life coach because these 12 plays are found in the greatest playbook of them all—the Bible. Godly men throughout the ages of the Bible have passed along these lessons. These lessons worked in the past. They work now. And they will continue to work for generations to come.

Now, are you ready to let me be your life coach? Great! Just turn the page and let's get started!

Knowing Who You Are

Basic Formation

Who are you trying to be, young brother? Yo, I don't mean what is your name. I mean, what do you want people to think about when they hear your name—Thug? Macho man? Dropout? Athlete? Baby Daddy? Scholar? What?

As a young African American male, you are presented with many images of manhood—some are negative and some are positive. In the long run, the most important challenge you will have to face in life is to figure out who you are.

Don't use your age as an excuse for not deciding the answer to this question. You're young. That means that this is the best time of your life to decide who you are. Why? Because you have the rest of your life to prepare.

You know Tiger Woods. He is the gold standard of excellence! Did you know that Tiger Woods was only 3 years old when he decided he wanted to be the greatest golfer in the world? Golf was so much in his mind and spirit at the age of 3 that he even appeared on a nationally televised talk show.

He didn't let his age or his African American heritage stop him from dreaming to become the best golfer ever. In the same way, don't you let your age or your race stop you from dreaming about who you want to become!

Blocking

You are not who people say you are. Don't let what others say about you tell you who you are. As I write this, I think of a young man at my school named Gary. Gary was a very smart boy. But for some reason he came to school each day with a chip on his shoulder. He was always fighting. He could never get along with anybody, even me. Every day I talked to Gary. I tried to convince him to get along with his brothers in school. Most of the staff tried to convince me to let Gary go. They told me that I couldn't save every boy. That made me more determined not to lose Gary!

I took him aside and had a heart to heart talk with him. He opened up to me. That's when I discovered that Gary had had very little encouragement in his young life. His dad was in prison. He lived with his mom. His mom was always telling him that he was "never going to be nothing." He internalized all of the negative things that were being said about him both at home and at school.

I asked him what he dreamed about himself. He thought for a minute. Then with his head bowed, he replied—almost in a whisper—that he wanted to become the President of the United States. What a mighty dream! Now that dream may or may not come true. But the important point here is that Gary had started to believe in himself. He said no to the negative things people were saying about him, and he began to dream about a good and hope-filled future. (Check out Jeremiah 29:11!)

Bootleg Pass

You are not like other people. Some young men try to act like the people around them. They might try to be like the head dog in class. Or they'll try to fit in with the tightest group in school. To do that they have to walk like them and talk like them. They have to wear the same name-brand shoes or jacket. They have to be like everyone but who they really *want* to be. They give in to what is called peer pressure. And giving in to peer pressure does not tell you who you are. It just tells people that you're like everybody else. But you are *not* like other people.

Fake Play

Sometimes, in a desire to convince others that they are different or special, young brothers will try to pretend to be someone they're not. They might disrupt class or wear something outrageous that will make them stand out in a crowd. Yet deep down inside they don't feel good about what they're doing. Why not? Because it's not really who they are. *If you have to pretend, then it's not you.*

Here's the good news: You don't have to pretend in order to be recognized as unique and special. All of us are already unique and special in God's eyes. That's the way we were created. Flaunt it—without fronting.

Goal Line

We know who you are not: You are not who people say you are. You are not like other people. You are also not who you pretend to be. When all is said and done, this is who you are: you are a child of God.

Does that sound crazy to you? It's true! In God's Word, we are told that "all who are led by the Spirit of God are children of God" (Romans 8:14-17). We are adopted into God's family when we choose to love and follow Jesus—and when Jesus becomes our big brother, then we can call God our dad. That's what the Bible means when it says we can call God "Abba" (verse 15). The Spirit of God assures us that we are children of God, "and if children, then heirs, heirs of God and joint heirs with Christ" (verse 17). An heir is someone who is entitled to share in everything that the parent has. And when God is that parent, you can count on some amazing rights—as well as some important responsibilities.

You see, recognizing that you are a child of God is just the starting place of developing a sound sense of identity—of figuring out exactly who you are. That is the starting point of developing a sound sense of identity. To be a child of God implies a certain character. Being a child of God implies a certain behavior. Who you are is not what you do. You don't need other people's approval. You don't have to be a copycat. You don't have to front for your peers. It is what you are inside yourself. You can be who you are and feel good about it.

Jesus knew who he was when he was twelve years old. When his parents found him in the temple talking to the elders, he said to them, "Did you not know that I must be in my Father's house?" (Luke 2:49). Jesus knew that he was the Son of God. And he knew that he was where he was supposed to be—in his Father's house.

The most important lesson in all of life is to know who you are. And when you understand that you are a child of God, then you have taken the first step on a mighty, mighty journey.

Basic Formation

List at least four different things that describe who you think you are.

- _____

- _____

- _____

- _____

- _____

Blocking

How would your friends and family describe you?

_____

_____

_____

_____

_____

Bootleg Pass

What kind of the peer pressure are you feeling in your life?

_____

_____

_____

_____

_____

Fake Play

List the times you behaved in ways that weren't really you.

- _____

_____

- _____

_____

- _____

_____

Goal Line

What does being a child of God mean to you?

_____

_____

_____

_____

_____

_____

_____

_____

_____

_____

_____

_____

_____

Knowing
Your Purpose

Basic Formation

Life has many challenges. If I asked you to name some right now, you might mention passing your weekly math quiz or making the cut on the school football team or controlling your temper. But I want to add one more to the list. I say that the greatest challenge you will ever have is trying to discover your purpose in life. That's right—*your purpose.*

Life is a gift from God. God wants you to live a good life and a long life. He wants you to enjoy your life. He wants you to be satisfied with your life. In order to do this, you must have the feeling that you're living for something. And that "something" is your purpose!

Without knowing your purpose, your life won't make much sense. You will get up each day without a plan. That's no good. Purpose is what gives meaning to your life. It gives you the feeling that you have something important, something good to do each and every day. Purpose gets you closer to your goal in life, whatever it is that you want to do in your future. After answering the question of who you are, knowing your purpose is the next most important play in your personal playbook!

Blocking

There are many adults who are still struggling to find their purpose in life. They didn't have someone in their life at a young age to challenge them to think long and strong about their purpose. Now they feel like their life doesn't count. They don't feel as happy as they want to feel. Why? Because they aren't sure they're doing what God put them here on earth to do.

What happens when young boys just like you are not coached on the importance of having a purpose in life? They are tempted to do destructive things that cheat themselves—or others—out of a future. They have no purpose, so they don't see that there's only prison and death in dealing drugs. They have no purpose, so they don't see that you shouldn't make a baby when you aren't prepared to be a father. They have no purpose, so they don't see that landing a job in today's world means going to college or getting some kind of advanced training after you finish high school.

So, young bro', how will you find *your* purpose?

Passing Play

To help you answer that, let's look at three young men who found their purpose in life. We'll start with a young man named Dwyane Wade. Brother Wade is a superstar basketball player for the Miami Heat. He's at the top of his game. Because of that, he was tapped to make a commercial for Lincoln Navigator. In this commercial he rides into a poor neighborhood where he sees a group of boys hanging out and making their own fun. He gets out of his Navigator and all eyes are on him. He yells to the boys, "I need some help!" Opening the door to his Navigator, he takes out a basketball hoop. Opening another door, a whole carload of basketballs roll out on the asphalt. Then he shoots the keys of the SUV to the coach, turns, and rides away on a bicycle.

In this commercial, Wade makes the statement, "My purpose in life is to leave the world a better place than I found it." His career as a basketball player lets him live a very comfortable lifestyle. His skills on the court even have young boys like you looking up to him as a role model. But he lives out his purpose of leaving the world a better place than he found it by bringing happiness to others who are less fortunate.

And guess what? He didn't have to wait until he was an "old man" to do it. Dwyane Wade was born on January 17, 1982. That means that when this book was published, he was only 26 years old!

So how do you want to help people? What do you want to do for people? One way to get at your purpose in life is to ignite a desire to leave the world a better place. You're not too young to start thinking about it right now!

Academy Formation

To help my students at Mays Academy focus on clarifying their purpose, I require them every day to repeat something known as the "Seven Rs Pledge." These are taken from a book by Ronald C. Mincy called *Nurturing Young Black Males*.* The seven Rs include respect, restraint, and most importantly, responsibility. The responsibility pledge is simple but powerful: "I will take RESPONSIBILITY for my conduct to give of my talents, my knowledge, and my skills to make the world a better place to live."

Try repeating this pledge each morning like my young Mays men do. Let's focus on our purpose together!

Offensive Formation

What's another way to figure out your purpose in life? *Start by identifying a problem and trying to solve it.*

The world will always have problems. People who distinguish themselves—who set themselves apart from the rest of the pack—are those who spend their life trying to solve a problem. They don't just sit back and complain. They rise up and actually do something to try and make things right.

Take Martin Luther King Jr. He tried to solve the problem of racial and economic injustice in our society. His powerful speeches addressed these themes and inspired the souls of folks across the globe. He rallied people together at nonviolent marches and sit-ins to call attention to the need for society to do something about injustice.

Although the problems of injustice still exist, the situation would be much worse if Dr. King had not decided that his purpose in life was to make the world a better place where all people are treated equally. And you know what? Dr. King was only 39 years old when he was assassinated. His influence still lives even though he never reached the age of 40!

Working to solve a problem gives you a feeling of fulfillment. It brings you a feeling of satisfaction—something that makes you want to shout "Yes!" while pumping your fist in the air. It gives you an inner confirmation that you have found the purpose for your life and you are living it.

Running Play

How you earn your living may also be how you accomplish your purpose in life. A lawyer wants to help people. He or she does it through the practice of law. A doctor wants to heal people and does it through the practice of medicine.

But there are situations where your career and your purpose in life may not be the same at all. Take, for example, a brother you might know as Jay-Z. He is president and chief executive officer of Def Jam Records. He is one of the founders of Roc-A-Fella Records. He is a producer who creates and markets the music of other rap artists. You might also know him as the rap star who spit "Show Me What You Got." He is one of the most successful rap artists working today. He has made a lot of money in his career in the music industry.

But something happened when he paid a visit to the African country of Angola. He saw something he had never seen before. He had grown up poor in America and thought he knew what poverty was all about. But when he got to Angola and saw children playing near open sewers filled with water contaminated by human waste and other filth, he changed. Realizing that these children didn't have clean water to drink or bathe in, he wanted to do something about this problem. *He wanted to bring clean water to the Angolan children.*

Jay-Z talked about his visit to Angola and what he had seen there in a video documentary called, *Diary of Jay-Z: Water for Life.* In that video he said, "In my business, we like to say we're from the hood. We're not from the hood. By no means. Not even close. How could I see this condition and do nothing about it?"* *

He was comparing the poor conditions under which he grew up to the awful conditions of the Angolan children who touched his heart and awakened within him a sense of purpose for his life. "How could I see this condition and do nothing about it?" Jay-Z found a problem—children not having clean water—and now he is working with other people to try and solve it. He works with the United Nations—the organization that works for world peace and also helps children around the world—and the cable television network MTV to try to make other young people aware of problems like those he saw in Angola. He found a problem and found his purpose. And guess what? Jay-Z is only 37 years old.

The Hook

Then there's Jesus. He was only 12 years old—maybe close to your age right now—when he publicly announced that he was aware of his purpose in life. In Luke 2:49, Jesus said, "I must be in my Father's house." The King James Version says, "I must be about my Father's business." At age 12, he may not have been clear about what his Father's business was or even how he would be involved in it. But this much *we* know—

The Father's business is helping people.
The Father's business is making the world a better place.
The Father's business is solving problems.

When Jesus got older, like Jay-Z, Jesus may have asked himself, "How could I see this condition and do nothing about it?"

He saw the problem of sin in the world and did something about it—he became the Savior of the world.

Goal Line

Let's look at one more point here. Martin Luther King Jr. was only 39 years old when he was called from us. Dwyane Wade is just 26 years old. Jay-Z is 37. Jesus was only 33 years old when he was crucified. I tell you the ages of these outstanding young men because they accomplished much while still very young. But you don't have to wait until you get to be their age to start thinking about the purpose for your life. You should start thinking about it now. The sooner you discover what your purpose in life is, the more time you can give yourself to doing it.

You may never have a national holiday named after you.

You may never be named a *Sports Illustrated* Sportsman of the Year.

You may never win a Grammy® award.

But knowing your purpose in life will be just as important as anything these young men have accomplished! So, find a problem and work to solve it. Find a wrong, and work to right it. There you have it—you've found your purpose. *Touchdown!*

Notes

* Ronald C. Mincy, ed., *Nurturing Young Black Males* (CEP Publications, 1994).
** You can view excerpts of the video documentary, *Diary of Jay-Z in Africa: Water for Life* (United Nations and MTV, 2006) at http://www.un.org/works/water/index.html.

Basic Formation

List four challenges that exist in your life right now. What could you do to overcome them?

- _____

  _____

- _____

  _____

- _____

  _____

- _____

  _____

Passing Play

Make a list of things you could do to leave the world a better place. How would you do them?

- _____

  _____

- _____

  _____

- _____

  _____

- _____

  _____

Offensive Formation

List four problems you see in your community. How would you solve them?

- _____

  _____

- _____

  _____

- _____

  _____

- _____

  _____

Running Play

Describe a time when you saw something that needed doing and you worked at it until it was done!

_____

_____

_____

_____

_____

_____

_____

_____

_____

The Value
of Education

Basic Formation

Education is perhaps the most valuable investment you can make in your life. I believe that so passionately that in August 1993, I opened the doors to a school just for boys. I named it the Benjamin E. Mays Male Academy. It is an elementary school with kindergarten through sixth grades. It was named for Dr. Benjamin E. Mays because for 27 years he was president of Morehouse College in Atlanta, Georgia. You may not know it, but Morehouse College is a mostly black all-male school!

As president of Morehouse College, Dr. Mays influenced hundreds of African American boys by impressing upon them the value of a quality education. To this day, some of the most affluent and influential African American men in this country are Morehouse graduates—including actor Samuel L. Jackson, director Spike Lee, pastors Calvin O. Butts and Otis Moss II, U. S. Surgeon General David Satcher, and Olympic gold medalist Edwin Moses. Dr. Martin Luther King Jr. is probably its most famous graduate. But Dr. Mays molded and shaped several generations of African American men.

One of the reasons I started the Mays Academy is because, like Dr. Mays, it gives me the opportunity to impress upon boys just like you how important it is to have a good education. Education is like a ladder that you climb step by step until you reach your goal.

Academy Formation

Every morning when my young "Mays men" assemble in what we call Formation before classes start, I emphasize certain lessons to them. These are lessons that I want to become a part of their character. I want these lessons to become their *backbone,* their inner strength.

The first lesson I want them to know is that they are at school. School is not a playground. School is that part of their world where they come to learn, to get knowledge, to absorb information, to answer questions, and discover answers to important questions about a wide range of topics.

I want my Mays men to understand that school is a serious place. Sure, it can be a fun place. Learning doesn't have to be boring. Learning can be fun! And I want them to enjoy learning. But learn they must. When I ask them, "Why are you here?" They respond in a booming, unified voice, "To learn, sir!" And that's just what I want them to say and remember. School is a place to learn.

Another lesson I impress upon my boys is that when they're in class, they must listen to their teacher. The purpose of class is to get knowledge. The teacher is in charge in the classroom. *And the teacher must be respected* because the teacher has the knowledge the student is there to get.

When they're in class, a Mays man is not to distract the teacher or any of his brothers. Why not? Because if he does, he breaks the rhythm and flow of giving and receiving knowledge. Gaining knowledge is an important time in a boy's day. It should not be interrupted by pranks or silliness by students who aren't there to learn.

Defensive Formation

I recall one incident in particular that made me so proud of my Mays men. A fourth-grade student transferred to Mays Academy from a local public school. I'll call him John. John had been expelled from his public school because he had behavioral problems. Nobody could get along with John. He was always acting out. He picked fights with other students every day. He turned desks over to disrupt the teacher. Over and over, he was sent to the principal's office, but he wouldn't accept discipline. His mother couldn't discipline him either. Finally, the principal at the public school had no choice but to permanently expel John.

Somehow John's mother found out about Mays Academy. We decided to give him a chance. When John came to our school, he tried to do the same things he had done at his other school:

- He disrupted the classroom.
- He rebelled against the teacher.
- He picked fights with other boys.
- He was constantly in and out of the principal's office.

Finally the Mays men in the fourth grade decided they were going to do something about John! One day they cornered him outside the classroom. They explained to him that his behavior was "un-Mays" behavior. They let him know that his acting out was unacceptable. They made it clear that they were in school to learn and that his behavior was interfering with their learning. They told him that if he didn't change his behavior, they would personally do what they had to do to have him dismissed from Mays Academy!

Their "little talk" worked. Soon after, John began to change his behavior. Before long, he fell in with the swing of things and became a good student:

- He started raising his hand before any of the other boys to answer a teacher's question.
- He fit in with the other boys.

- He accepted the authority of the teachers and the other adult staff.

- He got serious about his lessons.

I was proud of how the boys handled John. But I was most proud of the fact that they had grasped the lesson that I had been trying to impress upon them—that learning is important.

Passing Play

In African culture, the teacher is a revered and highly respected person. In fact, in earlier times, an African boy or girl looked up to the teacher as a god. The teacher-student relationship was sacred. The student understood that the teacher held the keys to unlocking the secrets and mysteries of life. Students were often called seekers because they were pursuing the knowledge possessed by the teacher.

Hanging on one of the walls of the Mays Academy are several African proverbs. One of them says, "Knowledge is better than riches." Now tell that to the rapper 50 Cent! He tries to teach you to "get rich or die trying." But the African proverb says, "Knowledge is better than riches." Why? Because knowledge is *the key to having all of the material things you want in life.*

Power Sweep

There is another lesson I stress to the Mays men each morning at Formation. After I ask them, "Why are you here?" and they shout back to me, "To learn, sir!" I ask, "Why do you learn?" And they answer, "Because knowledge is power!"

Knowledge is power! Yes, knowledge empowers you to get what you want out of life. Knowledge empowers you to accomplish your purpose in life. Without knowledge you will be ignorant and powerless. You don't want to be ignorant or powerless, do you? You are a person who wants to be able to get things honestly and make good things happen for yourself and other people.

Before I dismiss the Mays men to go to their morning classes, I place the tip of the forefinger of my right hand on the temple of the right side of my head. I don't have to say a word. My Mays men yell out, "Mays men are smart, sir!" That's what I want them to know and believe. They *are* smart! And so are you. *You* are smart! You just have to believe it and take time to prove it.

Tackle

Now while I believe that you are a smart young man, we do have a problem. You see, boys your age are dropping out of school at a rate so high it's scary! While dropout rates for other races are getting a little better, the dropout rate for African American males is increasing. *What's up with this?*

For some reason, our boys don't seem to get it. Your education is a huge part of your life. You cannot have the life you desire if you drop out of school. Dropping out of school is a sign that you have dropped out of life. When a boy drops out of school, he is much more likely to roam the streets. This leads to crime. Crime leads to prison or an early grave. Remember—when you drop out of school, you're flunking life.

Trap Play

For some reason, too many of our boys like the thug life. Do you want to be a thug? I meet a lot of our men who are intellectually gifted. They are really smart! They come from a good family where they receive love and support. They could make something outstanding out of themselves. But for some reason they're attracted to the thug life. They think being a thug is cool.

Being a thug is not cool! Thugs are a menace to society because they do not make the world in which they live a better place. They hurt people rather than help people. Thugs destroy things rather than create things. You want to be a thug? Just name me one thug who has made an outstanding contribution to the world.

Offensive Formation

When I was a boy your age, I wanted to be cool like the other boys. I wanted to dress and walk and talk just like the cool bruhs! But I had a life coach. Can you guess who he was? He was my father. My father taught me that God made me unique. He taught me that if I gave up my uniqueness the world would miss out on something God had intended for it to receive only through me. It was tough, I have to admit, but from my father—my life coach—*I learned to be myself.*

It takes courage and strength to be yourself. But in the end, it pays off.

It's part of growing up to want to be cool. You know, my generation invented cool just like your generation is into hip hop. But to be cool for my generation also meant being smart. That's right. Cool and smart go together. The last thing a boy in my generation wanted to do was flunk a class or flunk out of school. Flunking wasn't cool to us. Flunking hurt! We used to have a saying we would sing all the time, "Don't be no fool. Stay in school!" *That* was cool.

Bootleg Pass

Dissing school and making fun of classmates who do well in their lessons is something new in African American life. *It isn't a good thing.* I have boys tell me that because they like to read and score high on their math and science tests, other students tease them and say they're acting white. What? Listen up, young brother. Being smart is not acting white. Being smart is not acting anything. Being smart is being smart. Being smart is what you're supposed to be. You *are* smart. You're not dumb!

God gave you a brain just like everybody else. God expects you to develop your brain. That's what education is all about. You owe it to God, to yourself, and to your people to develop your brain.

Did you know that it used to be against the law for a black person to be caught reading? Did you know it used to be illegal to teach a black person to read and write? Too many people have given their lives and shed their blood, just so you could have the opportunity to go to school and learn to read and write.

Who will our doctors be? Who will provide health care to our people when they get sick? Why leave this important responsibility to someone else? Are we going to abandon the whole field of medicine because your generation believes that mastering math and science is acting white? I ask you to think seriously about this with me, little brother. You are our hope!

Hail Mary

Tell Dr. Benjamin Carson that mastering science is acting white. Do you know who he is? He is an African American considered by many people to be the greatest pediatric neurosurgeon in the world. A pediatric neurosurgeon operates on the brains of babies and children. And he is considered the best in the world!

His parents got a divorce when Carson was 8 years old, and after that he was raised by his mother. It was at that time that his grades began to slip. By the time he was in the fifth grade, he was doing so poorly in school that the other students called him "dummy." When his mother saw how poorly he was doing in school, she decided to help him improve. Even though she only had a third grade education herself, she made young Benjamin and his older brother read two books a week from the library and write book reports on each one. She also made them stop watching television (except for one quiz show).

It didn't take long for Benjamin Carson's teachers—and the other students—to start noticing the difference. In time he wasn't called "dummy" anymore. He was at the top of his class. With the dream of becoming a doctor, he went on to attend some of the best medical schools in the United States. In 1987 he did something that had never been done before—he operated to separate a pair of Siamese twins who were connected at the back of their heads. When other surgeons had tried to do this kind of operation, either one or both of the children had died. Dr. Carson succeeded when all others had failed. Now tell him that being a world famous surgeon who has saved the lives of many children is acting white! He is a gifted *human being*.

Or try telling Judge Greg Mathis that graduating from law school and being elected a judge in Michigan's 36th District Court is acting white. He is a former high school dropout and lawless teen. A judge ordered him to either go back to school and get his GED or go to jail. He made the right decision and chose school. He got his GED and then continued his journey by graduating from college. He became a committed public servant, working for a member of the Detroit City Council and later as manager of Detroit's system of neighborhood city halls under the legendary Mayor Coleman A. Young.

After graduating from law school he set his sights on becoming a judge. He was elected to that position in 1995. He is now nationally known and respected as the star of the *Judge Mathis* show! He dispenses justice fairly and shows that the law can indeed be colorblind.

Screen Pass

There are thousands of African American men who were once boys just like you. Many of them grew up in situations just like yours. They faced the same challenges and temptations that you face. They could have dropped out of school and even out of life. But they wanted to make something of themselves. They wanted to make their dreams come true. They wanted to thank the people who sacrificed so they could have the opportunity to go to school. Most of all, they wanted to make the world a better place for you. Join the team! Don't be ashamed of how smart you are. Go into the classroom and prove to yourself, your classmates, and your teacher that you are smart. I want you to do that.

Now that means you need to have a game plan:

- You'll have to turn off the television and get going on your homework.

- You'll have to read more than the chapters assigned by your teachers.

- You'll have to spend time at the library and stay on top of your academic game.

But you can do it. You *must* do it. America and the world are no longer black and white. You, my little brother, are going to have to compete with every nationality on the globe. In order to do that and be successful, you're going to have to have a good education. Do that for yourself. Nobody else can give it to you. You've got to get it for yourself.

Goal Line

Jesus was the smartest man who ever lived. At the age of 12, he was already engaging in intellectual conversations with the religious scholars and leaders of his day. He was always asking questions. He was inquisitive—he wanted to know about things. He wanted to understand life and God and the people of the world.

That's your assignment in the classroom. Like Jesus, be inquisitive. Ask questions until you understand the subject matter. Decide, like Dr. Benjamin Carson and Judge Greg Mathis, that you're going to be an expert in something and learn everything you can about it.

The Bible says that "Jesus increased in wisdom . . ." (Luke 2:52). Well, God expects you to do the same thing that Jesus did. God expects you to grow mentally and intellectually. He expects you to use your brain power. This is the role of education. It equips you with the intellectual tools you need to be the best man you can be.

Don't be a fool, young brother. Do your best in school!

Basic Formation

In addition to what you have read in this book, what other lessons have you learned about the importance of staying in school and learning all you can?

_____

_____

_____

_____

Who taught you those lessons?

_____

_____

Power Sweep

List some of the ways you believe knowledge is power.

- _____

- _____

- _____

Bootleg Pass

Whom do you know that disses school or disses you when you get good grades?

_____

_____

_____

What should you say to such people?

_____

_____

Hail Mary

List four people whom you admire and explain why.

• _____

_____

• _____

_____

• _____

_____

• _____

_____

What can you learn from each of their success stories?

• _____

_____

• _____

_____

• _____

_____

• _____

_____

A Man and His Money

Basic Formation

We live in a capitalistic society. This means that you are expected to prepare yourself to provide some service or sell some product to get money. Money is the most important material thing in the world. With it you can:

- acquire the things you want
- meet the obligations you will have
- help other people

Your challenge is going to be to learn how to get money—in an honest, legitimate way—and how to manage it when you get it.

Most of us are programmed to think that the way to get money is by getting a job. This is certainly one way to get money. But while you are young, I want to challenge you to start thinking in terms of starting and owning your own business. In other words, don't just think in terms of working for somebody. Think in terms of being in a position where people work for you.

Offensive Formation

In your neighborhood, jobs may be scarce and not many people may be able to hire you to work for them. In fact, black teenage unemployment is extremely high. In July 2007, more than 25 percent of black teenagers did not have a job. That means that one out of every four black teenagers who was looking for a summer job did not find one. Finding a job is not easy—especially for a boy your age, who isn't quite 16 years old.

Right now your parents or other caregivers probably give you money to get the things you want. But eventually, you'll want to have a means of getting your own money and doing for yourself. At your age, available work likely includes doing odd jobs such as running errands, doing yard work, babysitting, or shoveling snow. As you get older, more options will be available to you in retail, restaurant, and other industries. The first question, however, is where do you start?

Start by thinking of yourself as being a rich man. This is important because your attitude about money will have a lot to do with how you get it and how you use it. It is possible to think poor and end up poor. It is also possible to think rich and end up rich. *Learn early to develop a positive attitude about money!*

Academy Formation

To teach our Mays men about money, the Academy started a bank. The Mays men ran the bank. They elected the bank president. They also elected the members of the governing body of the bank, the board of the directors.

Each week the boys were required to perform some kind of task outside of school that they could be paid for. Specifically, they were required to develop a business and work as entrepreneurs (as their own bosses). They were to then bring the money to the Academy bank and deposit it. With this exercise they learned:

- how to save
- how to write a check

- how to balance a checkbook

- how to read a savings account statement

- how to compute the interest earned on their accounts

One of the most interesting aspects of this program was that the students learned how to apply for loans. After they developed a business idea, they had to complete an application for a loan and submit it to the bank's board of directors. The board of directors reviewed and then approved or denied the application. The board also had to justify their decision.

This gave the Mays men a new way of thinking about money and how to get it. This started them thinking about business ideas that they could handle themselves. One boy started a shoeshine business. He purchased some white plastic garbage bags and a black magic marker. He went to his church and asked the men each to take a garbage bag home and put their shoes in it. The young businessman wrote the name of each client on the outside of the appropriate bag. He took their shoes home, polished them, and brought them back the following Sunday.

Charging $5 for each pair of shoes, this young man created quite a brisk business for himself. In fact, his business grew so quickly that he had to hire a couple other boys to help him. He provided a needed service for the men at his church, and he got paid for it!

Running Play

You see, each boy devised a simple business venture. But the ventures gave these young men a chance to learn that making money starts with an idea. Don't ever disrespect your money-making ideas, no matter how far-fetched the concept might seem. Ask any wealthy person how he or she got rich and you'll hear that it all started with an idea. The Academy taught these Mays men how they can think in terms of creating a money-making business for themselves.

You can do the same thing. To earn money now, you can look around your neighborhood and see who runs the businesses. Go to the owner of a business. Introduce yourself. Tell him or her that you want to work. Establish that you're a good dedicated worker, and ask for a job. When you are hired, *do your job well.* At some point in time, ask the business owner to teach you how to run a business. Most business persons will be more than willing to take an interested and promising young person under their wing and teach you business principles that will help you earn a living and build a life.

Defensive Formation

Being exposed to these business principles at an early age is important because through them you will learn to earn dollars with dignity. You can't give in to the temptation to get involved with illegal practices to make money. Making money the honest way is still in style.

As a youth, you will be tempted to want everything right now. That's just a part of being young. But you're going to have to learn that you can't get everything now. It takes time to build a good life. You're going to have to resist the temptation to spend all of your money as soon as you get it.

Learn to save some of your money. Saving is a habit just like spending. To get started, go to a bank or credit union in your neighborhood. Ask one of the employees there how to open a savings account. Once you open your account, get in the habit of saving a little bit every week or month. Remember that it's not how much you deposit at any one time. The key is that you save *something* on a regular basis. As you work for your money and save some of it, you'll discover that your money will start working for you. That is what is happening when your money earns interest. Your money will begin to make money and increase the amount you started with!

How you manage your money will determine how you manage your life. Throw your money away and you're throwing your life away. Manage your money well and you'll manage your life well.

Trap Play

Learn now that going into debt is not good. Whatever you purchased still belongs to the person or store you bought it from until you have completely paid for it.

Sometimes it's hard to see the value of saving up for what we want because we want that item *right now*. Unfortunately, this hurry to spend our money usually leads us to spend it on things that don't have any real value. My grandson asked me to buy him a chain to wear around his neck. When I asked him why he wanted this chain, I discovered that he was really trying to impress his friends with his "bling bling." He wanted to be in style. His self-esteem was based on whether he dressed and looked like the other boys in his school.

My grandson was not alone. A lot of people make that same mistake. They spend their money on things that will impress other people and then they end up broke. Don't spend your money on things that do not have any long-term value.

Power Sweep

Saving for a college education has long-term value. Saving for a house has long-term value. These things will pay off for you over the course of your lifetime. They are good investments.

Think about your favorite pair of gym shoes. How much did they cost? Now find out what company makes that shoe. Find out what a share of stock in that company costs. I'll bet that a share of stock in the company is cheaper than a pair of their shoes! You should think in terms of buying a share of stock in that company instead of buying the running shoe first. The stock will earn money for you, but the shoes will wear out.

You can find out how much a share of stock in that company costs by asking your teacher to show you how to read the stock page in the newspaper. Or you can go to you neighborhood bank and ask the manager to look it up for you. Better yet, find the company's information on the Internet. If you don't have access to a computer at home, just go to your local public library. The librarians are trained to help you.

Goal Line

Believe it or not, money is spiritual. I say this because money has the power to do a lot of the things that we pray and ask God to do for us. Perhaps for that reason, money competes for our commitment and devotion to God. It is possible for people to get so much money that they begin to believe that they don't need God. I don't ever want you to get to the point where you begin to think about money so much that you put it in place of God in your life.

Oprah Winfrey has made a lot of money, but she doesn't just spend her money on herself. She also uses it to help other people. Recently she spent a lot of her money to build a school and housing complex for poor girls in South Africa. This is what God wants all of us to learn. As the Lord blesses us with money, he also wants us to be a blessing to others.

Did you realize that God is the source of getting money? There is a Scripture that says: "But remember the LORD your God, for it is he who gives you power to get wealth . . ." (Deuteronomy 8:18). God gives you life. God gives you health and strength. And God gives you the ability to get money. Once we get money, however, the Lord wants us to use it to take care of ourselves and to make the world a better place.

YOUR PRIVATE PLAYBOOK

Running Play

List four moneymaking ideas you could start right now.

- _____
- _____
- _____
- _____

Now, pick one and make a plan for getting it started.

_____

_____

_____

_____

_____

Defensive Formation

What are some of the things you would like to save money for? How much money will you need to afford each one?

- _____
- _____
- _____
- _____
- _____
- _____

How long do you think you'll have to save in order to have enough money for each one?

_____

_____

Trap Play

What are some of the things you want *right now* that you know don't have any long-term value?

- _____

- _____

- _____

Power Sweep

What company would you like to own stock in? How much per share is that company's stock worth?

_____

_____

Research that company. Find out as much about it as you can, and record what you learn here.

_____

_____

_____

_____

_____

_____

Dealing
with Parents

Basic Formation

No person has the privilege of choosing the family into which he or she is born. No mother gets her child's permission to give birth. One day each of us just opens our eyes, lets out a wail, and—ready or not world—here we are!

God gave each of us the gift of life. No matter how pleasant or unpleasant we may feel about the circumstances into which we were born, all of us have the challenge of making the best we can of our lives.

In a perfect world, from the day of your birth onward, your parents—mother and father both—will continue to express their love for you by doing their best to provide for your physical needs and to create an atmosphere in your home where you can feel loved, wanted, and respected. *Parents are called by God to do only what is best for their children.*

But we are not living in a perfect world. I can no longer assume that you live in a family with your father, your mother, and your brothers and sisters. The family unit as we used to think of it is fading as an accurate depiction of family. You may live with just one of your parents and some of your siblings. It is possible that your "parents" are not your biological mother and father at all. Perhaps you are being raised by your grandmother, your aunt and uncle, or a cousin. Maybe you are in a foster home or have been adopted by loving parents who have made you their son— but whom you know aren't your birth mother and father. Perhaps learning to love them and feel as if you are part of a caring family is extremely challenging and difficult for you.

No matter what your situation, it is safe to say that no one has a perfect home and no one has perfect parents. It is also safe to say that, for better or worse, there will be no greater influence in your life than your parents, guardian, or other caregiver. And for better or worse, the Bible recognizes the cost required to bring a child into the world and raise him or her to adulthood, and God instructs us to honor our parents—those who gave birth to us and those who are raising us—for our own good.

Huddle

Whatever your family looks like, it is within that family that you learn your first life lessons—the lessons that will determine the kind of person you will be. In the family, you learn to respect authority. Your parents are the first authority figures in your life. Part of their job is to teach you how to behave so when you are away from home you will know how to interact with other people. Following your family's rules of social behavior is important because it will help you learn the self-discipline needed to follow similar rules in other environments—at school, in the movie theater, at the mall, or on the job.

Also, parents should teach you the importance of good grooming. They are supposed to make you brush your teeth, clean your ears, wash up, and dress neatly. They may even have to remind you to put a comb to your hair or lotion on your skin! That is because your appearance is important. It may not seem fair, but people will make judgments about you based upon your appearance. When your parents stress the importance of good grooming, they do so because they want you to make a positive impression on other people.

All families have rules for the house. For instance, your mother might insist that when you get up in the morning you make up your bed and straighten up your room. Your father might expect you to take out the trash and help with the laundry. Your grandmother might require you to set and clear the table at mealtimes. By doing these things, your parents are trying to teach you the values of being a disciplined and responsible person. When you learn to be responsible for yourself, you won't blame others for what you should be doing yourself.

You will not always understand *why* your parents make the decisions they make. But they have the larger responsibility of looking out for the welfare of the entire family. So, whatever your parents' rules may be—and whether you understand them or not—you should respect and obey them. When you respect rules at home, you learn to respect rules everywhere. If you refuse to accept the rules and authority of your parents, you will not respect rules and authority anywhere. Always remember that there are consequences for breaking the rules. These consequences can be severe and may change your life forever!

Academy Formation

At Mays Academy, we have what we call the "Three Ships of the Academy." They are *scholarship, leadership,* and *citizenship.* In explaining to Mays men what is meant by citizenship, we tell them that wherever they go, there are rules. Whether they are at home, walking at the mall, on the playground, in church, or in a classroom, *there are expected rules of behavior.*

Mays men are told that wherever they are, it is their responsibility to:

- *know* the rules
- *understand* the rules
- *obey* the rules

Going by the rules keeps you from getting in trouble with people in authority. People in authority are responsible for enforcing the rules.

Bootleg Pass

As you enter the teenage years, something happens. You have probably already begun to question your parents' decisions. You might begin to think you are smarter then they are. You may look at your parents as being old-fashioned and out of it. Like most youth your age, you start listening to your peers and believe they know better than your parents what you should and should not do.

Being increasingly influenced by your friends, dressing like them, enjoying the same music and activities, and having fun together is part of growing up. Parents understand this because—believe it or not—they were once young like you and they went through the same thing!

Going along with your peers is a part of feeling like a normal guy and being accepted as a part of the group. And you are at a point in your life when being accepted as a part of the group is important. Being ridiculed or rejected hurts, no matter how old you are. But at your age, such rejection might make you begin to think that something is wrong with you. *Nothing is wrong with you!* It's just a part of growing up.

Defensive Formation

That being said, you must also know that no matter how cool they are, your friends aren't always right. In fact, in the name of fun, your peers will sometimes do things they know are wrong just to see if they can get away with it.

This is where you have to draw the line. Remember the good and honorable lessons your parents have taught you. Obey their rules. Good and godly parents—more than your peers—have your best interests at heart.

If they are trying to raise you according to God's Word and to what is right, then your parents ought to be your primary role models. A role model is a person of character who is faithful in carrying out their responsibilities.

You may admire the basketball skills of LeBron James. You may even be impressed by how he carries himself. And, hey, there's definitely nothing wrong with learning skills that improve your game from somebody who's better at it than you are. But no matter how great an athlete may be at a sport, that athlete is not your role model.

A role model is somebody you want to pattern your life after. It should be somebody you know and have a relationship with. That's why I say your parents are your role models.

There is nothing wrong with emulating the best qualities in other people. But when it comes to choosing a role model, look at the example your parents have set. If your parents are not the kind of people God would have you emulate, look around to other members of your family, your church, or your community. Find someone whose character is godly and whose behavior is worthy of respect and imitation. Then model that person's character and faithfulness.

Running Play

As I acknowledged earlier, you may be growing up in a home with only one parent. In most cases, it's your mother. You aren't alone. In fact, the 2005 U. S. Census reports that almost 37 percent of black youth under the age of eighteen live in a household headed by a female. That's more than one-third of young people just like you!

For any number of reasons, your father may be absent. Your mother can still set a good example for you to follow. I have often heard successful men praise their mother. These are men who are athletes, businessmen, engineers, teachers, doctors—men who grew up in a one-parent family in the hard environment of the inner city. They are grateful for their mother's hard work, sacrifice, and firm discipline. These grateful sons credit their mother for their success!

Goal Line

One of the first lessons the Bible teaches us about the parent-child relationship is found in Exodus 20:12, which says, "Honor your father and your mother, so that your days may be long. . . ." Why would God attach the promise of long life to this command to honor your parents? Because the instruction and direction of your parents, if received and obeyed, will steer you out of harm's way and onto a productive path of living.

We are to honor our parents because they gave us life. Life is a gift from God that he gives us through our parents. It's said that even Jesus, who *was* perfect, was obedient to his parents (Luke 2:51). Jesus is our example. If he was obedient to his parents, we should be obedient to our parents as well. Honoring your parents and being obedient to them is God's will for your life.

Basic Formation

List some of the first lessons your parents (or caregivers) taught you. Why is each one important?

- _____

- _____

- _____

- _____

- _____

What are some of your parents' (or caregivers') rules?

- _____

- _____

- _____

- _____

- _____

Why are these rules important?

_____

_____

_____

What happens when you don't obey them?

_____

_____

Bootleg Pass

Make a list of your tightest friends.

- _____

- _____

- _____

- _____

When have they tried to get you to do something you knew you shouldn't do?

_____

_____

How did you respond? What did you do? Why?

_____

_____

_____

_____

Goal Line

List some of the ways in which you can honor your parents (or caregivers).

- _____

- _____

- _____

- _____

- _____

The Boys
and the Girls

Basic Formation

My grandson is 9 years old and starting to get inquisitive about girls. Not too long ago, he asked me how old I was the first time I kissed a girl. "I don't remember!" I told him, but asked him if he had ever kissed a girl. By the look on his face I could tell he found the thought to be quite offensive!

As the conversation continued, I asked him, "Who is the prettiest girl you've ever seen?" He told me her name. I'll call her Mary. When he got his nerve up to tell Mary that he liked her, she said she liked him too.

"What did you do when she said she liked you?" I asked him.

"I went in the bathroom and looked in the mirror and said, 'I can't believe Mary likes me too!'"

He looks at her in class, he says, but when she looks back at him he can't take it. "Her eyes always get the best of me!"

I would say that all young brothers have been where my grandson is now. But I know that it won't be much longer before his shyness wears off and he becomes more serious about girls.

Since the beginning of time, the so-called opposite sex has always exercised a great deal of influence on us as men. When we are growing into manhood, we don't quite know how to handle the feelings girls inspire in us.

Academy Formation

Do you know why I wanted to have a school just for boys? One reason is that girls in the classroom can be a distraction. Boys want to impress girls so badly that they can lose focus on what the teacher is talking about. Instead, they give their attention to the girls. That's a problem when one of our primary goals at the Academy is education!

What's more, boys love to compete. And they often compete with each other for the attention of the girls. In some cases, competition can even escalate into a fight. This is a distraction our Mays men cannot afford, not when we try to emphasize teamwork and responsibility for one another.

Tackle

Reaching the age of puberty causes you to change physically and emotionally. Hormones begin to rage, causing you to:

- Produce testosterone
- Become more aggressive
- Grow physically
- Experience changes in your voice
- Grow hair on your face and in your pubic area
- Become sexually aroused

At this stage in your development, you begin to look at girls differently. You become sexually curious, and you may even begin to pursue girls just to see if you can score. Sexual conquests become part of your thinking about what it means to be a male.

The flaw in this kind of thinking is that it leads you to believe that the more girls you get over with sexually, the more of a "man" you are. Some men hold on to this idea about manhood even into their adult life!

This is a critical time in your development. You are beginning to form your definition of what it means to be a man. You will also begin to form your definition of what a woman is. What you believe about girls at this point in your life is very probably what you will believe about women as an adult. How you treat them now establishes a pattern for how you treat them later. Therefore, this stage of your development is crucially important for both you and your future spouse and children!

Trap Play

If you only think of girls as sexual conquests, you will never be able to develop a healthy relationship with a woman. You won't see her as a person but as someone whose only purpose is to fulfill your sexual desires. That is a serious issue confronting your generation—for boys and girls alike!

In many of the lyrics of popular rap artists, women are referred to as "hoes" and "bitches." These are loaded terms that undermine the humanity of the woman. When men use such negative language about women, it undermines the possibility of entering into a healthy relationship with one another. You can't think of yourself as a person while thinking of her as an object. *"Thingifying" a woman also "thingifies" you!*

Pursuing girls as sexual conquests has other real dangers. The more sexually active you become, the more you run the risk of getting an STD—sexually transmitted disease. This is no small problem. Sex can kill you! HIV/AIDS is spreading more rapidly among African American teens and young adults than any other group in the United States—because of this casual attitude about sexual relationships.

If you only think of girls as sexual conquests, you'll never be able to develop a healthy relationship with a woman. You will reduce her and yourself to mere "things," not deserving respect or love. And you may very well put your own and others' lives at stake by exposing yourself to disease.

Fake Pass

Another risk you take when you pursue girls as sexual conquests is that you might get her pregnant. When you bring a baby into the world before you or the girl are emotionally and economically prepared, that causes serious challenges for the families involved—especially the girl's family. In most cases, it is her family that has to take the economic hit and raise the child. The boy usually runs away. He becomes just another "baby daddy." His family is seldom there for emotional and economic support. This is unfair to the child, the girl, and her family—as well as to the boy who may grow up to be a man who regrets his youthful immaturity and irresponsibility.

God made men and women to have two different functions in the sexual relationship. The man bears the seed; the woman nurtures the seed. Another reason to take your sexuality seriously is because your sperm is sacred. Yes, that's right! Because life is sacred, sperm—which is the seed of life—is also sacred. It is a gift God has given you to be able to produce life.

That is what we teach our Mays men. As a seed-bearer, young brother, you must not be irresponsible. Producing a life is serious business. Learn to practice principle over passion!

Offensive Formation

At some point, you're going to be smitten by a girl. You're going to feel some emotions that you won't understand. Guess what? It's okay. It's natural. It's human. That's what happens between boys and girls. While you're young, learn to own your feelings. Don't deny them. Work at becoming comfortable with your feelings and how to express them.

This is a time in your life to grow emotionally. As boys, you get mixed messages about how to handle your feelings. You are told that "big boys don't cry." You are led to believe that crying is a sign of weakness. This is not true. In the appropriate context, crying can be a sign of maturity and of a well-adjusted, emotionally healthy person.

You are told that boys and men aren't supposed to feel. You're supposed to be cold, hard, logical, and unaffected by emotion. This is just nonsense. All human beings experience a full range of emotions. You can feel love as well as anger. You can be gentle as well as strong. And the more comfortable you become with your own feelings, the more comfortable you will be in interacting with girls!

Understand that girls are God's creation too. Male and female were together created in God's image. Therefore, neither boys nor girls are superior or inferior to the other. Respect girls as people.

When you respect them, girls can be good friends just like your best male friends. When you share common interests, you discover that you have a lot to talk about and a lot of things you can enjoy together.

It's best to develop a friendship first and then let the relationship evolve. The important task for you at this point in your life it to see girls as humans, not as objects of sexual conquest. Become comfortable relating to girls with no motive other than to enjoy your relationship with them.

Goal Line

More than once, I've had a Mays man ask me, "How do you choose a girl?" Adult men have asked me this question, too. It is not an easy question to answer. You must know that developing and sustaining a healthy, strong relationship isn't easy. It doesn't happen by magic. It happens because two people commit themselves to God and to each other to make it work.

In searching for an answer to this question, however, I found a model in Genesis 2:21-22, the story of Adam and Eve—the first boy and girl. The Bible says that God put Adam to sleep, split him in the side, took out one of his ribs, and stitched him back up. Now just imagine Adam lying there on God's operating table, face up. Then imagine that with Adam's rib, God makes a woman. She too is on God's operating table, lying face up right beside Adam.

In that posture, I see five points of contact that I suggest be taken in serious consideration as you choose a girlfriend. I call it the Five Areas of Compatibility.

1. **Physical attraction.** Physical attraction may bring the two of you together initially, but "pretty" and "fine" are not qualities on which to build and sustain a relationship. Looks change, after all. Physical *interaction* will always be a part of the relationship, but physical *attraction* alone is not enough to build a life.

2. **Intellectual compatibility.** This means that you share common interests. You can talk about things that are of interest to you both. This keeps you from becoming bored with the other person.

3. **Spiritual and emotional compatibility.** The heart symbolizes what you share in common values. You should have similar beliefs, especially religious beliefs. It's better if both of you share a common faith and enjoy going to church.

4. **Work and productivity.** The hands suggest that you are working to achieve common goals. You can't be working for one goal and she another. Together, you must be moving in the same direction, using your shared resources to achieve those goals. This allows you to *celebrate* together what you *achieve* together.

5. **Social compatibility.** I associate this area with the feet because socially, you like to go to the same places and do the same things. Companionship is the reason you enter into a relationship. It's no fun if you have to do the things you like to do alone.

Keep in mind, even at this young age: You have a life to build, and the person who stands by your side and travels with you should be more than a showpiece. As Genesis 2 describes the role of Eve in Adam's life, your future spouse should be a helper. She should be a person who can help you reach your potential, reach your goals, and reach your destiny.

Tackle

List the changes you have noticed in yourself—physically and emotionally.

- _____

- _____

- _____

- _____

- _____

How do you feel about each of those changes?

_____

_____

_____

_____

_____

Offensive Formation

How would you like to see yourself grow and mature in your friendships or relationships with girls?

_____

_____

_____

_____

_____

Goal Line

Look at each of the Five Areas of Compatibility. Write down your personal comments about each one:

1. Physical attraction

_____

_____

_____

2. Intellectual compatibility

_____

_____

_____

3. Spiritual and emotional compatibility

_____

_____

_____

4. Work and productivity

_____

_____

_____

5. Social compatibility

_____

_____

_____

Friendship—
Our Brother's Keeper

Basic Formation

An old proverb says, "Tell me the company you keep, and I'll tell you who you are." Watching the company you keep is important because, as the proverb implies, it says a *whole* lot about you. You see, what you admire in others, you usually wish for yourself.

Choose your friends carefully and wisely. Everybody who pretends to be your friend is not. And if you are not selective in your choice of friends, you could end up being deceived, hurt, and even embarrassed. Choose as your friends boys who reflect the same ambition to succeed as you do and who seem to have the best qualities that you possess or desire to imitate.

Trap Play

Charles (not his real name) was a fine boy. He had two sisters and a younger brother. By the time school was out each day, Charles's mother had not gotten off from work. Charles's responsibility was to watch his two sisters and little brother until their mother got home.

At school, Charles was part of a group of four boys. They were his friends. One afternoon, they persuaded Charles to leave his sisters and brother alone to hang out with them. They assured him that they would get back before his mother got home. Reluctantly, Charles went along, partly to be with his friends but also to prove his friendship. He jumped into the car with them, not knowing that it was a stolen car and that one of the other boys had brought along a gun.

The boy who was driving the car didn't even have a driver's license, but he was in a show-offish mood. So feeling a little too much like Batman, he careened around a corner and slammed into some parked cars. Afraid, he drove away from the scene, but before he got too far away, the police chased him down and pulled the car over.

After asking the boys to get out of the car, the officers searched the car and found the gun. All four boys were taken to the police station and charged with driving a stolen car and possession of a firearm.

Charles hadn't bargained for all of this! He had thought that he would just hang out for a little while with his friends and return home to watch his sisters and brother before his mother got home. You can imagine how upset and disappointed Mom was when she did get home.

The Hook

I found out about this incident because Charles came to me for a character reference. The prosecutor in the case was going to recommend a sentence of a few weeks of community service. As part of my agreement to write the character reference (I have known Charles all of his life), I made him agree to do his community service at my church and under my direct supervision— if the prosecutor approved of this arrangement. Charles agreed. The prosecutor agreed.

I used this situation to teach Charles several life lessons, but the main one was about friends and friendship. Charles made a mistake when he allowed his friends to persuade him to leave his responsibilities. His mother was depending on him. His sisters and brother needed him. Can people depend on *you* to do what you say you will do?

Fake Pass

Friendship is not just about the other person. Friendship also has to do with the kind of friend *you* will be. In this instance, Charles's loyalty to his friends was greater than his loyalty to his family. That was not unusual. At your age, loyalty to friends often supersedes loyalty to the family. That's called peer pressure. Parents constantly complain that their child's friends have more influence over their child than they do as parents.

While loyalty is the glue that holds friends together, you do *not* have to be loyal to friends who want you to do wrong just to prove your loyalty. In fact, *the friend who wants you to help them do wrong is no friend at all.* When Charles explained to his friends that he had to stay home to watch his sisters and brother until his mother got home, that should have been enough for his friends. Instead, they kept leaning on him until he caved in to their pressure.

Tackle

Too many young brothers are ruining their lives or ending up in prison because they have no limits on their loyalty to people who aren't deserving of such uncritical allegiance. Far too often their loyalty is to somebody who has a negative influence on them.

Wanting to belong to a group is a natural part of the socialization experience—the process through which you learn to get along with people and find where you fit into different groups. But you have to make a choice about which group you will and will not belong to. Remember the proverb at the beginning of this chapter. The group you choose to belong to says something—and sometimes *everything*—about the kind of person you are. To quote another proverb, "Birds of a feather flock together."

Charles's experience frightened him. He had never been in trouble with the police before. Going to jail, needing to get a lawyer, facing a prosecutor and a judge—that was serious business. For Charles it was a life-altering experience. This incident shook him up! He kept insisting to me that he was innocent. "I didn't steal the car. It wasn't my gun." He felt he was being treated unfairly.

Bootleg Pass

Technically, Charles was *not* guilty of either of these unfortunate offenses. I even believe the prosecutor knew that, too. Charles's problem was that he was with the persons who were guilty. This incident will appear on his record for a period of time because he is *guilty by association.*

This is how a whole lot of young brothers start traveling down the wrong path. They may not be guilty the first time. But show up the wrong place at the wrong time too many times and it's no accident. It establishes a pattern of behavior that becomes a forecast of the future that the boy is shaping for himself.

There's a price to be paid for choosing to belong to the wrong group. Rightly or wrongly, you *are* judged by the company you keep. If your friends are doing something today, people will believe that you might do it tomorrow. As Ice Cube of NWA said, "You better check yourself before you wreck yourself."

What do you suppose Charles's mother thought about his friends? She probably didn't have a very good opinion of them after she saw her son fall under their bad influence. That's why good parents want to know who your friends are. Mom and Dad or Grandma or Auntie can't be with you 24/7. They want the comfort of knowing that the person or group you're hanging with is having a *positive* effect on you.

Defensive Formation

Out of this incident Charles and I grew closer. I would say we became friends. An older man *can* be a friend to a younger man. Sometimes younger men need the input and insight of an older man. If your father is around, that's the role he should play in your life. He should be there to give you certain information about how to navigate the growth passages in your life. He should be there to tell you how to handle certain situations so that you can come out of them still feeling like your male pride is intact.

If you do not have a relationship with your father or if your dad is unlikely to offer a positive role model himself, there might be other older males in your family to whom you can turn—an uncle, a grandfather, or an adult cousin. Seek their insight and advice from time to time. There are a lot of good men in the churches in your neighborhood as well. Go to church. Seek out positive places and positive people.

Screen Pass

As Charles and I grew closer, he shared some private thoughts with me about himself and his family. They were thoughts that I honestly believe he had never told anybody else. He told me that he had once contemplated suicide. When I asked him why he would think such a thing, he told me that he felt poor and dirty and that no one cared about him. He felt his friends always had money and the hottest shoes and clothes. He couldn't keep up with them. He felt like he was a burden to his mother and that she would be better off without him around.

Those were deep personal thoughts that he shared with me, and I just listened without arguing or preaching or judging. That's the opportunity that a good friendship creates. A good friend listens to you. He is a person to whom you can trust your most personal thoughts without fear of being condemned or reprimanded. A good friend tries to understand you.

Blocking

Second Samuel 13 records the story about King David's son Amnon, who rapes his sister, Tamar. As bad as the incident was itself, the problem began when Amnon told his friend Jonadab about his lust for his sister. Instead of giving Amnon *good* advice and discouraging him from doing such a terrible thing, Jonadab gave him the plan to rape Tamar. That story specifically states in verse 3 that Jonadab was Amnon's friend. Amnon shared his personal, private thoughts, but a so-called friend gave him some bad advice.

Real friends don't help you do wrong. Real friends listen without judging you, but if they see you making a bad choice or going in the wrong direction, they warn you and discourage you from taking that path. They will encourage you to do what's right.

If you mess up on your own, a real friend doesn't diss you or abandon you. Charles had messed up. And even though he usually didn't hang with me, when he needed my help, I was there. I could have pushed him aside and kicked him to the curb. But I chose to stand by him in his worst moment. A real friend will do that.

Passing Play

Sometimes a friendship comes out of nowhere. I call these "accidental friendships." By this I mean that you weren't necessarily intending to develop a friendship with this person. But something happens that brings the two of you together and you end up friends.

This could happen with you. Maybe somebody sees that you're good in math. He may ask for your help studying for a test, and when you take a break, you discover that you both like the same music or enjoy the same hobby. And in that moment, a friendship begins. You weren't looking for a new friend. It's just that somebody reached out to you and it gave you the opportunity to *be* a friend. In that kind of situation, help the person in need without expecting anything in return—and be open to finding a new friend "by accident."

Goal Line

Proverbs 27:17 says, "Iron sharpens iron, and one person sharpens the wits of another." This means that a good friendship improves both people. You help him be a better person, and he helps you be a better person. And there's nothing wrong with a little healthy competition among friends. When you compete as friends and not as rivals, you each improve yourself. You can also bond with each other, in victory and defeat, and you will be able to celebrate each other's progress.

At the Mays Academy, we try to encourage this understanding of friendship. We want our Mays men to have healthy competition. So they study together. They drill each other over the questions they think will be on the next test. When the test is over, they compare scores. For the next exam, they commit themselves to perform better than the one who got the highest grade. This is "iron sharpening iron." This is brother improving brother. This is a friend being a friend.

At the Academy we enforce what we call Rule #1. The boys repeat it every day:

- No hitting
- No kicking
- No bullying
- No fighting
- Brothers don't fight brothers
- Brothers help brothers, sir!

Basic Formation

Who are your closest friends?

- _____

- _____

- _____

How are they like you?

_____

_____

_____

_____

How are they different from you?

_____

_____

_____

_____

Trap Play

When has a friend ever tried to get you to do something you shouldn't do?

_____

_____

_____

What did you do, and why did you make that decision?

_____

_____

_____

_____

_____

Goal Line

How have you helped a friend be a better person?

_____

_____

_____

_____

How has a friend helped you be a better person?

_____

_____

_____

_____

_____

_____

There Is a
Leader in You

Basic Formation

The values and habits you are forming today are shaping you into the man you're going to be in the future. While that may not seem important to you now, you should take some time and reflect on your young life. Look at your habits and look at your values. Get a better idea about the kind of person you are and the kind of person you are becoming.

I can tell you that over the course of your life, you will change many times. You will drop some habits and pick up new ones. Some things that are important to you now won't be as important to you later on.

Like all of us, you are growing. An important part of the growth process is self-reflection for the purpose of self-evaluation. Your goal in this process is to become the best person you can be—by learning to confront yourself, to be honest with yourself, and to hold yourself accountable.

The Hook

As a child of God, the standard by which you should evaluate yourself is Jesus. In all things, he is our perfect example. Never evaluate yourself against another human being, no matter how little or how much you may admire them. Doing so will give you a false estimate of yourself.

If you don't think much of the person, you will overvalue yourself. When you do this, you will make excuses for your shortcomings by saying things like, "Well, at least I'm not as bad as Johnny."

When you think highly of a person, you won't give yourself enough credit. You will make statements like, "I will never be as good as Johnny."

Just as it was in Jesus' parable of the talents (read it in Matthew 25:24-28), there will always be people who will be more on the ball than you are. There will also be some who will be less on the ball than you are. The point is to be the best *you* can be. You will only succeed at that by evaluating yourself over and against Jesus' perfect example. No other standard will do.

Blocking

In this self-evaluation process, most people underestimate themselves. I see boys all the time who do that. For example, too many have convinced themselves that they can't do math—even before they try it! "It's too hard," they say. However, when they are challenged to try anyway and when they commit themselves to making the effort, they discover that math isn't as hard as they had convinced themselves it was.

This same dynamic operates in other areas of life, whether it relates to trying out for the JV squad or the school play or to speaking in front of an audience or asking a girl to a local dance. We convince ourselves that we can't do things before we even try them.

I don't want you to underestimate yourself, little brother. You can do more than you believe you can. You have more going for you than you realize. *There is a leader in you!* You have the potential to be a pacesetter. You have the potential to call the shots. When people underestimate themselves, they give up their leadership and follow someone else just because they have never learned to believe in themselves.

So, don't underestimate yourself. Get in touch with the leadership instincts inside of you. Begin by setting a standard for yourself, and then work to achieve it. When you accomplish the personal goals you have set for yourself, you separate yourself from the pack. Before you know it, you become the standard by which others measure themselves. This is what leaders do. They set the standard for others to live up to.

Think of any person you consider a great leader. Can you see that part of their lasting appeal is the high standard they set that is respected by others?

Academy Formation

In Play #5, I mentioned that at the Mays Academy we stress the Three Ships of the Academy. I told you that we call them scholarship, leadership, and citizenship. I emphasized citizenship in that chapter. But here I want to emphasize *leadership*.

Mays men are taught that they are leaders and not followers. They are to respond to the best impulses within themselves. They are not to give unquestioned allegiance to anyone. They do not blindly go along to get along.

Each week we award the Adhama Vest to the boy who is recommended by the staff to be the Mays Man of the Week. (*Adhama* is a Swahili term for glory and honor.) The boy who is awarded the Adhama Vest gets to lead in all group activities for the week and to give out all the group commands.

This is one way we try to develop leadership within the Mays men, not only by recognizing them for their potential but also by allowing them to experience how it feels to be in charge.

Power Sweep

Exercising leadership qualities *now* will open up greater opportunities to you for service later on in life. And make no mistake, young brothers, leadership is not just about being the boss and calling the shots; leadership is about service. Leadership is not contained in a title you wear or a position you hold but *in the service you render*.

Here's an example of what I mean. A young brother named Rahim lived in an apartment complex. During the coldest month of the year, the heat went out. The adults in the building tried their best to contact the landlord to get the heat turned back on, but they had no success. It got so cold that some tenants had to leave their apartments and move in with relatives or friends. Others who didn't have anywhere else to go bought space heaters, put on more clothes, and wrapped up in blankets.

Rahim decided to do something about the situation. He organized the kids in the complex. They contacted a local television station and succeeded in getting their story in an evening newscast. As spokesperson for the young people, Rahim explained—on the air—how their parents had tried with no success to contact the landlord. He went on to say that, as kids, they were freezing and getting sick and struggling to do their homework because of the cold. They needed the heat turned back on!

As you might expect, when that story hit the airwaves, things got done. The landlord suddenly showed up and got the heat turned back on. Thanks to Rahim's leadership, a problem was resolved!

Rahim exercised his leadership by organizing the kids in the complex, bringing a serious problem to the public's attention, and getting the problem resolved for his family and his neighbors. *Leaders render service.* That's what Jesus meant when he said, "Whoever wishes to become great among you must be your servant" (Mark 10:43).

Trap Play

This is a different perspective on leadership than the world has. The world thinks of leadership as winning—achieving the goal or prize first. The problem is that leadership that focuses on winning can be mean-spirited, cold, and callous. For example, a focus on winning can cause businesses to think more about profits than about people. To increase their profits, a business may have to dismiss thousands of employees with no regard for how those people are going to earn money to pay their bills and take care of their families.

The danger of equating leadership with winning is that some people don't care *how* they win just so long as they *win*. This may lead to cheating. In fact, I've even heard some sportscasters say, "If you're not cheating, you're not trying." Well, there's something wrong with that statement. Cheating is wrong whether it's in sports, business, or anywhere else in life!

Fake Pass

In thinking about leadership as serving others, you must be compassionate—you have to care about people. And, you must have *character*. Having character means that you are who you say you are. You have probably seen how some of our national leaders embarrassed themselves—and even ruined their careers—because they publicly said one thing and got caught doing something else! You have to be who you say you are, or you will be known as someone who does not have character.

Goal Line

Leaders do what they say they're going to do. They keep their word. They answer to the people they are leading. You will keep the public's respect and confidence only if you show that you know what you're doing and have nothing to hide.

The world needs good, trustworthy leaders. There are too many problems out there waiting for someone to take initiative in solving them. While we often look to elected leaders to solve our problems for us, those officials can only do so much. What's more, their issue may not be your issue. They may not know or care about the things that are important to you. That's why leadership, even (and especially) at a young age, is critical if you hope to make the world in which we live a better place.

When all is said and done, a leader is someone who doesn't rely on someone else to make the first move. Any person who leads is, by definition, a leader. So, if you see that there's something that needs to be done, don't just sit back and wait for somebody else to do it. Get up and do it yourself. That's what a leader does!

Basic Formation

Make a list of the kinds of things that are important to you in life.

- _____
- _____
- _____
- _____
- _____

Now describe yourself based upon that list.

_____
_____
_____
_____
_____

Power Sweep

Describe a situation in your school, church, or neighborhood where you would like to exercise servant leadership.

_____
_____
_____
_____
_____

Now create a service plan that describes how you will address the problem.

_____

_____

_____

_____

_____

Goal Line

List the needs you see on a local, national, and international level.

- _____

- _____

- _____

- _____

- _____

Now, list the ways you think you can address those needs by providing leadership service in the future.

_____

_____

_____

_____

_____

_____

When Things Don't Work the Way You Expected

Basic Formation

You're probably already acquainted with disappointment. It's one of the spoilers in the game of life. You can have your life's game plan in place. You can have your personal goal line in view. Then disappointment will step out from the sidelines, blitz you, throw you for a loss, and leave you facing fourth and long.

No matter what age you are at this time, you have already experienced disappointment. There was something you wanted for Christmas that you didn't get. Maybe you tried out for JV and didn't make the team. Even worse, maybe your friend got shot and killed in a senseless argument.

Disappointment is a major player in the game of life. It sacks your hopes and dreams. No matter how noble your dreams, no matter how pure your aspirations—the reality is that things don't always work out the way you hope they would.

Defensive Formation

You may not know it, but you have already begun to develop a strategy for dealing with disappointment. What did you do when you didn't get that special item for Christmas? What did you do when you didn't make the team? How did you handle it when your friend was slaughtered?

Did you get mad and reject what you *did* receive? Did you quit practicing and trying to improve your skills? Did you harden your heart and seek revenge? How have you dealt with disappointment so far? It's important to think about the answer to that question because you will need a strategy for dealing with disappointment that you can use the rest of your life.

Blocking

Disappointment can have a negative effect on your life when it keeps you from trying to do the things you've set out to do. In times of disappointment, this is where:

- Your willpower is tested

- Your inner strength is revealed

- Your resilience—your ability to bounce back—is formed

- Your determination is put front and center

If you allow life's disappointments to discourage you, you'll give up. You won't try. And you'll end up a loser.

Losers are people who quit trying. If you quit trying you can't win; you can't achieve your goals; you can't realize your dreams. In order to succeed, you must always believe that you can win. Don't worry about how wide the gap is in the score or how much time is left on the clock. If you're behind, you must still play the game as if you believe that not only can you catch up, but you can win the game!

Trap Play

Some people allow disappointment to fill them with a victim or "poor me" mentality. They cry, "Everybody is against me." They make excuses: "It wasn't my fault." They give up: "I tried. It's no use!" And in the end, they let life happen *to* them rather than make life happen *for* them.

But learn this—you can respond to disappointment in one of two ways. You can cave in and let life happen *to* you. Or you can regroup and make life happen *for* you.

Here's a true story. I know a young man who was an out-standing college athlete. Before he reached his junior year, he decided that he would pursue eligibility for the draft. Sure enough, he was a high draft pick in the first round of the NFL. He started out great. He looked like he was going to be the superstar he had always dreamed he would be.

Then, halfway through his rookie season, he suffered a season-ending injury. While recovering, he began to do casual drugs with some old friends from his boyhood days. When he returned to the team, a drug test showed illegal drugs in his system. He was suspended for the number of games required by the league. He also had to pay a fine. More than that, when he returned to the field, something was different. Something was missing from his playing skills. Another draft choice beat him out for his position.

He responded to this huge disappointment by getting angry and playing the victim. He said things like, "The coach never wanted me on the team anyway." About the player who beat him out for his position, he declared, "He's not as fast as I am. His hands aren't as sure as mine. They just want him 'cause he acts white."

To have such tremendous talent and have to sit on the bench *is* a huge disappointment. But to blame everybody else for what you did or failed to do is *not* the way to handle it.

This brother dealt with disappointment by allowing it to create in him a "victim" mentality. A victim mentality says, "I'm not to blame. People are doing this *to* me." It's hard to win when you feel like a victim. Even if you do win, when you have a victim mentality you probably feel like you don't deserve the victory and cannot enjoy it.

Offensive Formation

The first thing you must do to deal with disappointment is to face it with an *overcomer's* spirit. So this young man experienced a season-ending injury. What if he hadn't become so lazy while he was healing? What if, instead of doing drugs, he had focused on overcoming by strengthening his body and by improving his game? It's possible that upon his return to the field, he might have had a different outcome.

It's important for you to understand that things won't always work out the way you think they should. But don't cave in to disappointment. Be an overcomer!

Running Play

There's no clear path between where you are and where you're trying to go. You'll run into obstacles and be forced to take detours. Follow the detour and keep on going. A detour means only that it may take you longer than you expected to get where you're trying to go. A detour never means that you won't get there!

There may be roadblocks along your way. These are meant to destroy your resilience. Don't let that happen! Overcome the disappointment and keep on going.

Tackle

Eventually my young friend came face to face with another disappointment. He got cut from the team altogether. That's right—they let him go! This was a major disappointment. All of his life he'd had but one dream and that was to be a star in the NFL. He got his chance, but now it was over before he had really gotten started.

As sad as his story was up to this point, it got worse. No other team picked him up. He tried out for several other teams, but none of them wanted him. Now, that was a major disappointment! He had to rethink his whole life's game plan, and he was faced with a decision. He had to decide how to deal with this latest disappointment. He could continue to play the victim, or he could suck it up and get on with his life. You see, disappointment may stop you temporarily, but you must never allow it to defeat you.

This young man wallowed in his misery for a while, but then he began to see life from a different perspective. He became an overcomer. He went back to college, got his degree, and landed a job coaching a middle-school football team. He overcame his disappointment and went on with his life.

Hook

Sometimes disappointment is God's way of getting you where he's trying to take you. When I think of disappointment, I always remember Joseph. You know Joseph—the Joseph from Genesis 37–50. Those chapters tell about Joseph's experiences with disappointment and how he handled each one as it came his way.

Joseph had high hopes and great expectations for himself, but he experienced disappointment from within his family. He shared his life dream with his brothers, and they responded with angry jealousy. They got so mad that they decided to get rid of him altogether by selling him into slavery! You see, disappointment doesn't always come from strangers or outside sources. Disappointment can sometimes come from within your own family. You might expect encouragement from your family, but it's not always there. Parents and siblings don't always feel your dream. That is what Joseph experienced. But in spite of it, he held on to his dream.

If disappointment can strip you of your dream, you're finished. Things won't always work out the way you want, but hang on to your dream!

Bootleg Pass

While in slavery, Joseph was purchased by a man named Potiphar. He was captain of the Egyptian army. Joseph was his servant—his handyman and personal attendant. But Potiphar's wife put Joseph in a bind. She tried to force Joseph to have sex with her, but he refused. Because he wouldn't, the woman lied to her husband and accused Joseph of raping her. When Potiphar heard this, he put Joseph in prison.

Sometimes disappointment goes from bad to worse. Joseph had dreams, but his brothers sold him into slavery and then his master, Potiphar, put him in prison. Joseph had dreams, but it looked like he was going down.

Power Sweep

Joseph could have become discouraged and given up, but he didn't. He held on to his dream. In whatever situation he found himself, he improved his skills and nurtured his faith in God. As long as you have a dream that you're pursuing, you're a winner. But if disappointment and discouragement make you abandon your dream, you lose.

Eventually Joseph ended up as the head of the Department of Housing and Human Services of Egypt, second in command only to Pharaoh himself. He could never have arrived at that position if he had let his skills—and his faith—die.

My friend is still in football. He's not the superstar he had hoped to be, but he teaches his skills to kids whose dreams are just beginning to form. From his personal experience, he can teach them what pitfalls to avoid in pursuing those dreams and how to deal with disappointment along the way. He may never have gotten this opportunity if he had not learned how to overcome his own disappointment.

Goal Line

No matter what disappointment you face, keep developing your talents. The door of opportunity may slam shut in your face for now, but it will open again later on in life. And when it does, you have to be ready. So, don't stop improving your skills, whatever they may be. Be ready for that second chance!

Joseph faced years of disappointment, but he never lost his faith in God. He kept praying. He held on to his faith. And in time, God opened doors for him to fulfill those youthful dreams—in a leadership position that served the nation of Egypt and its neighboring countries as well. The same principles can work for you. No matter how hopeless it looks for you, keep on praying, keep on hoping, and keep on trusting. Somehow, some-way—sooner or later—God will see you through.

Basic Formation

List some of the major disappointments in your life.

- _____

- _____

- _____

How did you handle each one?

_____

_____

_____

Offensive Formation

How would you handle these disappointments differently now—with an overcomer's spirit?

_____

_____

_____

Power Sweep

Which people in your life have overcome disappointment? What were their disappointments, and how did they overcome them?

_____

_____

_____

Running Play

List some of your goals in life.

- _____

- _____

- _____

- _____

- _____

For each goal, list what you think might be some of the road-blocks or detours to reaching those goals.

- _____

- _____

- _____

- _____

- _____

Now, describe ways you would prevent discouragement from keeping you from those goals.

_____

_____

_____

_____

_____

_____

Your Body Is the Temple of God

Basic Formation

By this time in your life, you are no doubt into your body. You're growing physically. Your shoe size has changed. You're getting taller. You're getting heavier, adding muscle where you used to be just skin, bone, and baby fat. Not only that, but the development of hormones in your body is changing how you feel about yourself.

Puberty is a time when your body goes through many changes. You become aware of your sexuality. Your voice gets deeper, and you start sounding like a man. Hair grows in the pubic area, and peach fuzz grows on your face. All of these changes are a natural and normal part of the growth process. You are being physically prepared for adulthood.

Passing Play

Psychologically, you are developing an attitude about your body. Not long ago a frantic mother of a fourth grade student called me. She calmed down long enough to explain the reason for her call: She had arrived home from work to find that her son had taken a razor blade and shaved his eyebrows off. A chill went through me just imagining it. Can you imagine how this mother felt? She went on to explain that when she asked him why he would do such a thing, her son said he was ugly and that the kids at school always made fun of him.

Now Tony (not his real name) is a good-looking boy whose thick eyebrows are a part of his handsome looks. But because his eyebrows are bushier then average, he thinks something is wrong with him. It isn't important what his mother or I or anyone else thinks. What's important is what he thinks about how he looks.

For the most part, your body shape and size are determined by your DNA (the information stored in your genes, which you inherit from your biological parents). How you feel about what you see when you look in the mirror, however, is up to you. And for some reason, a lot of boys don't feel good about their bodies. They think they're too short or too tall. They're too skinny or too fat. They're too dark-skinned or too light-skinned. For most of us, accepting our body comes in time as we mature into manhood. But for some of us, that acceptance is a long time in coming!

Fake Pass

The issue of self-acceptance can be even more difficult for black boys because at this age you also begin to feel the historical weight of racism. This legacy of injustice has created a number of negative stereotypes about black males that influence your self-acceptance, whether you're aware of the effect or not.

Racist stereotypes portray black boys as being "animalistic," with brute strength. They are characterized as being over-sexed and possessed with a criminal nature. Even the term *black* in our often racist culture refers to something negative, bad, and inferior. Among African Americans ourselves, we might call another black person "a black so and so"—and *black* in that context is meant to be a put-down. Or we may say that another black person has "nappy" hair, implying that because it isn't stringy and straight like a white person's hair, such hair is inferior. All of this and more is left to us as part of the legacy of racism.

Defensive Formation

These negative images will affect your image of yourself. You have to be a strong and special person to fight off the temptation to believe what other people say about you. *But you're going to have to do it.*

Being tall does not mean that you have to be a basketball player. Similarly, you do not have to play football just because you may be a big fella. Now there's nothing wrong with excelling in either of these sports. (I had a little game myself back in the day!) I'm only saying that *it is your choice.* Do not allow your body type to force you into "stereotypical" thinking.

Consider the student who graduated from the Mays Academy and enrolled in a prestigious private school in the area. He was big for his age. He was also an excellent student. After a few days at his new school, it became clear that the white coaches and student athletes were trying to coax him into joining the football team. He told them that he played football for recreation, but that he was a scholar. Their response was, "Oh, okay, scholar (snicker, snicker)."

Here was a black boy who wanted to excel academically. Because he had a strong physical presence, many people wanted to view him only as an athlete. But he was focused on his brain power. This young man is now a pre-med student on an academic scholarship at an outstanding university!

Don't believe the stereotypes when you look at yourself in the mirror. Accept yourself and how you look. But be the person *you* want to be, not the person other people think you should be.

The Hook

Your body is the most marvelous machine that was ever created. There's nothing superfluous or unnecessary about it. God made it in such a perfect, compact way that it has everything you need to do whatever you want to accomplish in life. It is designed for the long-distance journey. But to go the distance in life, you'll need to enjoy good health. And that means you'll have to start taking care of your body *now*.

I want you to start focusing on your body and your health because, unfortunately, black men have a shorter lifespan than men in other racial groups. At least part of the reason for this is because too many men don't take care of their bodies like they should. But you can live the long, rewarding life God has designed for you by reversing this trend.

To reverse it, first you have to be aware that the problem exists. Second, you must know what to do about it. And third, you must then *do* it.

Blocking

Black men die from high blood pressure, heart disease, prostate cancer, colon cancer, and gun violence at rates much higher than the average American citizen. There are a number of reasons for this. One reason these health conditions exist is related to some men's idea of what being a man is.

For example, some men don't get their prostate or colon checked because of where these organs are located in the body and the way the testing instruments must go into the body. They think of the procedures as an invasion of their manhood. Nonsense! These are just tests. Consenting to them has nothing to do with being a man or not being a man. The physical examination needs to be done to make sure you're healthy. In fact, because early detection is so important in these diseases, the exams can even save your life.

Another reason for the high rates of certain diseases among black men is that too many men don't go to the doctor until they get really sick. This is also part of that so-called macho mentality. These men think they're tough and figure they can handle the symptoms. And so they put up with the pain and discomfort until it's too late. These men haven't developed a healthy pattern of getting regular check-ups.

When your body is not functioning as it should, it tries to tell you something's wrong. That's what symptoms such as pain and fever indicate—an emergency signal from your body. So when you feel something wrong in your body, get it checked out. If you find a disease early, in most cases it can be cured!

However, you can't have a disease diagnosed if you won't go to the doctor. Be sure that you feel comfortable with your physician. You might prefer to find an African American doctor. Some doctors of other races aren't always as sensitive in relating to a black man as they should be. Whichever doctor your choose, however, find one that you are comfortable talking to. You should feel at ease telling him or her anything that is affecting your body, no matter how personal. Doctors know the functions of all the organs of the body. You won't embarrass your physician by talking about any part of your body, nor should you be embarrassed by asking questions. It's your body. Take care of it!

Trap Play

Diet—what you do or don't eat—plays a role in the poor health of too many black men. Racism in our society has created the 'hood. If you live in the 'hood, life is rough. Sometimes you don't have enough money to buy the right foods from the right food groups. The grocery stores in the 'hood don't always stock the fresh fruits and vegetables, dairy products, and meats you need to have a balanced, healthy diet. Too often, eating what *is* readily available means that you aren't getting healthy meals. Black men need to be careful about getting foods that are too high in fat, salt, and sugar—just because those things are easy to come by and taste good.

Lifestyle also plays a role in this. You've probably seen too many black men who are just couch potatoes. They park themselves in front of the television (often with junk food close at hand) until it's time to roll over into bed. They haven't developed an exercise routine.

Other economic factors lead to the poor health status of some black men. Many don't have health insurance or the money to purchase it. Even those who do have enough insurance to *see* the doctor don't have the money to buy the prescribed medicine.

Maybe you noticed that among the physical ailments I listed above, I included gun violence in the causes of death for black men. Life in the 'hood is violent. And violence is a health risk. Primarily, black boys and men are the one who commit violent acts against each other. Young brother, packing a gun doesn't make you a man. Flashing a knife doesn't make you a man. Solving fights with your fists or another weapon does not make you a man. Committing any act of violence does not make you a man. Violence just puts you in prison—or the morgue.

For all of these reasons and more—and I encourage you to do some research on your own—black men are not getting enough quality living out of their bodies.

Power Sweep

You, young brother, can help reverse this trend! To do that, I want to introduce you to a concept that I hope you will adopt today and allow it to shape your thinking about your body and your health. It isn't an original thought. It comes from the Bible. In 1 Corinthians 6:19, the apostle Paul writes, "Do you not know that your body is a temple of the Holy Spirit within you, which you have from God, and that you are not your own?"

I want you to think of your body as the temple of God. Thinking this way will give you a new view about your body—a view that is completely different from the perspective you pick up in the streets. It will make you more aware of how to take care of your body properly. In other words, it will make you more health conscious.

Your body belongs to God. You are the manager of your body, but God is the owner. This is a different way of thinking about your body—a healthier way. God gave you this body so you would have an instrument with which to do the work you were created to do. It is the physical tool God gave you to accomplish your work in the world. Take care of it, and it will take care of you. Neglect it, and it will let you down.

Your body is the temple of God. This means that your body is sacred. It is not to be used like a trash can. You're not to dump garbage inside your body. Unhealthy food—high in fat, salt, and sugar—can be turned into garbage in your body. Careless and casual sex is garbage—and you risk adding the additional trash of STDs. Steroids, illegal drugs, alcohol, cigarette smoke—all of these things are garbage. You may think that using these things socially makes you look cool, but physically, you're destroying your body.

When you dump garbage in your body, you're just planting the seeds of disease in yourself. Ultimately, these things cause your body to break down and stop working properly. Trash takes its toll and turns what God intended to be a temple into a garbage dump. (Did you know that the word used in Matthew's Gospel for hell is *Gehenna,* which was the name for the garbage heap outside Jerusalem where the Jewish people burned their trash?)

Goal Line

There's one more thing. Scripture tells us that your body is the temple of God *because God is in you.* This is what Paul meant by the phrase "the Holy Spirit which is in you." In the ancient world, a temple was a building constructed as a home for a god or for the spirit of that god. Your body has been given to you so that it can be the dwelling place of God's Spirit. God wants you to project physically his Spirit and his goodness. In doing so, you will discover health, vitality, and happiness. God wants you to be strong and healthy. He wants you to project an image of prosperity and well being.

Of course, some of us were born with an illness or an affliction. God will give you the strength to bear that too. In fact, in his letter to the Christians in Rome, Paul says, "We also boast in our sufferings, knowing that suffering produces endurance, and endurance produces character, and character produces hope, and hope does not disappoint us, because God's love has been poured into our hearts through the Holy Spirit that has been given to us" (Romans 5:3-5). In other words, when we persevere—hold on to our dreams and our faith even in physical disappointment and suffering—God can redeem something good out of that difficulty.

Another important thing to remember is that if, to the best of your ability, you take care of the body God has given you, then at some point, your efforts will open up opportunities for you. One of those might be an opportunity to share with others what you know about the importance of thinking of the body as the temple of God.

So, take care of your body and enjoy the measure of good health God has given you. Learn to see your body as the temple of God, and allow that perspective to give you a new frame of reference to relate to how your body may be changing—and how it may stay the same! Hopefully, this will inspire you to become more health conscious and ultimately give you a more satisfying life.

YOUR PRIVATE PLAYBOOK

Basic Formation

How would you describe your body?

_____

_____

_____

_____

_____

In what ways have you felt uncomfortable about your body, and why?

_____

_____

_____

_____

_____

How can you overcome these feelings?

_____

_____

_____

_____

_____

_____

Power Sweep

What kinds of changes can you make to show that your body is a temple that belongs to God?

- _____

_____

- _____

_____

- _____

_____

- _____

_____

How can you help others understand that their body is the temple of God?

_____

_____

_____

_____

_____

_____

_____

_____

_____

_____

Shouldering Your Social Responsibility

Basic Formation

Any person who is blessed to achieve some level of success should feel a sense of responsibility to reach back and try to help somebody else. No matter who that person is or what he or she has accomplished, that person achieved that position of success through the help of somebody else.

Remember this—you can't make it by yourself. You need the help and support of others. They might encourage you just by giving you a pat on the back to let you know that you've done a good job. Or they might put in a good word for you with someone who's looking to hire some good workers. Whatever the help may be, *nobody makes it alone.*

Trap Play

In recent years, a number of high-profile black athletes and professionals have come under serious criticism. Why? Because they have chosen *not* to use their position, wealth, and influence to make a difference in the lives of others. You see, many of these people came from very humble beginnings themselves. They may have lived in extreme poverty. Or they may have had a troubled or nonexistent family life. But they escaped the hazards of the 'hood. Their talent and hard work pushed them to the very top of their chosen career paths.

Now that they have made it, they live a comfortable, even lavish, lifestyle. They appear to be satisfied with what they've accomplished. But many of them seem to feel no need to reach back and inspire young people to rise up and overcome conditions like the very ones they escaped! They seem to have adopted an "I've got mine, you get yours" attitude. Sadly, a number of these successful individuals have even gotten involved in activities that have landed them in jail. These people are in a position to do a lot of good, but instead they have set a bad example for the scores of youth who—rightly or wrongly—look up to them as role models.

Running Play

There is an old saying: "Don't let your ability carry you where your character can't keep you." Character is important. It defines what kind of person you are. No matter where you set out to go in life, you must decide what kind of person you're going to be. Under no circumstance do you want to set a bad example for others to follow.

This is where *social responsibility* begins. It begins simply by being a good person, willing to help others. Everybody can be a good person. Not everyone will necessarily be an activist or lead a great movement for social change. But everyone has the chance to be a person of good character.

A man modeling good character before his family, his neighbors, and his coworkers is being socially responsible. He is setting a positive example that can be modeled by young boys who will aspire to grow up and be just like him. But social responsibility goes beyond being a good and honorable person. It is also using your position and influence as you become involved in activities that have some socially redeeming value. Starting now, become involved in activities that help others.

Academy Formation

At the Mays Academy, we teach our Mays men that the true purpose of education is not merely to prepare them to get a good job, make a lot of money, and live a comfortable life. Those things in themselves aren't bad. But beyond this, Mays men are expected to ask themselves, "What social problem can I try to solve?"

This is a question you should begin to ask yourself now and continue to ask over the course of your life. For example, your question might be, "Who will inspire black boys to choose books over guns?" It might be, "What will convince people to address the AIDS crisis in Africa?" It might be, "How can our community help solve the problem of homelessness?" Raising questions about social problems will gradually stir up within you a desire to do something about that problem.

Screen Pass

Taking initiative to do something about a problem is one way to be socially responsible. Of course, it is natural to feel a problem is so big that there isn't *anything* you can do about it. But never underestimate yourself and the contribution you can make to solving that problem. Some effort is better than none. Doing something is better than doing nothing. Remember, if you're not a part of the solution, you're a part of the problem!

Tackle

Sometimes we don't think about a problem until it affects us personally. The basketball great Magic Johnson may be a little old school for you, but for me, during my late teen and young adult years, he was—as far as athletes go—a hero. During his years with the Los Angeles Lakers, he was called "The Playmaker." He made dazzling passes and mind-blowing shots. He was the Floor General who unselfishly moved the ball among his teammates. He had a will to win. More than that, he refused to lose.

That's why it was a shock to the world when he called a press conference one morning to announce that he was retiring from the NBA because he had been diagnosed as HIV positive. He had the virus that can become AIDS. A stellar career was coming to a nightmare end.

This wasn't the way Magic was supposed to go out. Holding back tears and fighting through embarrassment, he bravely explained that he had been "recklessly promiscuous." *Reckless* meant that when he decided that he was not going to save sex for marriage, he had unprotected sex (sex without a condom). *Promiscuous* meant that he had had sex with a lot of different women. Now both his recklessness and promiscuity had come back to haunt him in the worst of all ways.

Hail Mary

Magic could have disappeared quietly from the public stage and retreated to hold on to his health. Instead, he became a spokesperson for AIDS prevention. He traveled all over the country warning young people about the consequences of unprotected sexual behavior. By telling them about his own mistakes, he showed them that the best way—God's way—is abstinence (not having sex until you're married).

Instead of being a part of the problem by becoming just another statistic, Magic Johnson decided to use his experience, his position, and his influence to become a part of the solution. Magic is a powerful example of how someone has tried to bring some social responsibility to a problem that still affects us. The problem came to Magic, and rather than giving in to it, he responded by doing something about it.

You cannot predict what may inspire you to become involved in a socially responsible activity. My purpose here is to plant in your spirit the idea that you can do something to transform society. You can choose a problem and attack it, or as in the case of Magic Johnson and many others, a problem may choose you. In either case, it's better to do something about that problem than to do nothing.

Power Sweep

There are many unknown and unsung heroes. In every community, there are people who do things they don't have to do. They do what they do just because it's *right*. I am thinking now of the countless church workers who give their time and talent to work with youth groups, Scout troops, senior citizens, and more. There are scores of people who volunteer at their community hospitals, organize a neighborhood block club, or lead a protest against a powerful company because of unfair hiring practices.

Being socially responsible does not always mean gaining publicity so that other people know what you're doing. More often than not, social responsibility means doing what you do, not to be seen or honored, but because it's the right thing to do. All of us benefit from the efforts of people we'll never know. The world is a decent place to live because, quietly and faithfully, millions of unsung heroes labor in their own corner of the world to transform society.

Goal Line

In one of his parables, Jesus explained how God rewards us. In Matthew 25:31-35, he described how God rewarded those who fed him when he was hungry, clothed him when he was naked, and visited him when he was in prison. They were confused and asked, "When did we see you hungry or naked or in prison?" God's response to them was, "When you did it to the least among you, you did it to me."

This was Jesus' way of telling us that when we quietly and faithfully do something to help others—with no motive except that it is the right thing to do—we are rewarded by God. Don't forget this lesson. God sees what you do. God knows why you do it. And God rewards what you do. There is no greater satisfaction then receiving God's reward.

Basic Formation

List four times others have helped or supported *you* when they didn't have to.

- _____
- _____
- _____
- _____

List four times you have helped or supported *others* when you didn't have to.

- _____
- _____
- _____
- _____

Running Play

Describe the kind of person you hope to be as an adult.

_____

_____

_____

_____

_____

_____

_____

In what ways do you hope to be socially responsible?

_____

_____

_____

In what ways are you being socially responsible now?

_____

_____

_____

Power Sweep

List some of the things "unknown" heroes have done in your community to make it a better place.

- _____

- _____

- _____

- _____

- _____

Why is receiving God's reward for what you do better than receiving a reward from other people?

_____

_____

_____

_____

Leaving
a Legacy

Basic Formation

You're never too young to think about how you want to be remembered. When people call your name, what image do you want to come to mind? What thoughts do you want them to think about? What emotions do you want to stir inside of them? What memories do you want to evoke?

These are important questions. Why? Because how you respond reveals what you want others to think about your life. You should start thinking about these questions now because doing so will help you point your life in a certain direction. Don't just walk aimlessly into the future. Dream of a future you want for yourself, and *live your life in that direction.*

Power Sweep

It's not enough to think about what you want to get out of life. It's just as important—if not more so—to think about what you want to give back to life. You don't just want to live. You want your life to count for something. Whatever that "something" is will be your legacy.

Whether we recognize it or not, all of us leave a legacy. Some people—the ones who live more in the public eye—are more widely known for the legacy they leave. Their contributions are more widely publicized. Others aren't known except by the few lives they touch. Nevertheless, they still leave a legacy.

Running Play

Tyrell was only 7 years old when he died. He was born with a rare disease that affected his lungs. Doctors did everything they could to give Tyrell some relief and a chance to live. But for all their best efforts, every breath was still a struggle for this little fella.

The doctors had only given Tyrell a year or two to live, three years at the most. His mother was determined to see a miracle for her baby. She took him to several out-of-state hospitals to see if anybody could save him, but the report of all of the doctors was the same. The miracle was that he had lived as long as he did.

I remember his mother saying at his funeral service, "Don't cry for us. God gave me Tyrell to teach me the meaning of joy and the beauty of life. He was here for just a short time, but he taught me so much." Do you get it? You never knew Tyrell. The world never knew Tyrell. But for those who did know him, he left a legacy: "He taught me the meaning of joy and the beauty of life."

The Hook

Naturally, all of us want to leave a positive legacy. But remember, what people think about your legacy—how they interpret it—isn't up to you. Others will determine the significance and meaning of your legacy. Some will like what you've tried to do and some won't. But you can't live for the opinion of others.

You must live out of a conviction and commitment to whatever your core values are. Although everyone wants to be well thought of, don't worry too much about that. You won't be able to please everyone. *Just be true to yourself.*

Offensive Formation

Having said this, I want to share certain principles that you can consider over the course of your life as it relates to leaving a legacy.

First, leave a personal example worthy of respect. Each person is unique and designed by God to make a special contribution. You bring a lot to the table of life. Use it to set a good example.

Second, morally and spiritually, live on such a high level that others will be so attracted to and inspired by you that they'll want to imitate—not *your* life—but the *kind* of life that you lead.

Third, whatever your job is, do it so well that others work harder and improve the quality of their own work. Raise the bar by your personal example.

Fourth, use your talents, your influence, and your voice to speak for those who cannot speak for themselves.

Fifth, there is a situation with your name on it. It will come to you. Don't run away from it. You will discover that God has equipped you with the ability to change that situation and make it better.

Sixth, strive to love your family and develop a relationship with them. Then when you aren't with them anymore, they'll miss you. In this way, you put yourself in their hearts.

Seventh, when all is said and done, the bottom line of life is relationships. Be at ease with all kinds of people; it takes all kinds to make the world. Try to understand people more than you want them to understand you. Be loving and caring. Don't be judgmental. Give more to others than you expect from them.

Goal Line—Touchdown!

Finally, young brother, remember Jesus. He lived so well that, to this very day, the mention of his name makes us aware of the areas in our lives where we know we can do better. At the same time, he was so warm and caring that people to this day still sing, "What a Friend We Have in Jesus." Try to be that kind of friend to everyone with whom you have a relationship.

In all things, Jesus should be your example. If you pattern your life after him, you'll leave the world a legacy of a life well lived. It's an example the world needs. I invite you, young brother, to make this your life's quest!

> If then there is any encouragement in Christ, any consolation from love, any sharing in the Spirit, any compassion and sympathy, make my joy complete: be of the same mind, having the same love, being in full accord and of one mind. Do nothing from selfish ambition or conceit, but in humility regard others as better than yourselves. Let each of you look not to your own interests, but to the interests of others. Let the same mind be in you that was in Christ Jesus . . .
>
> —Philippians 2:1-5

Basic Formation

What are some of your dreams for your future?

- _____

_____

- _____

_____

- _____

_____

Power Sweep

List some of the blessings in your life.

- _____

- _____

- _____

- _____

- _____

How can you use those blessings to give back to others?

_____

_____

_____

_____

_____

Offensive Formation

Describe some of the unique gifts God has given you.

_____

_____

_____

_____

How will you use them?

_____

_____

_____

_____

Goal Line—Touchdown!

In what ways would you like to pattern your life after Jesus?

_____

_____

_____

_____

How will this help you leave your legacy?

_____

_____

_____

_____

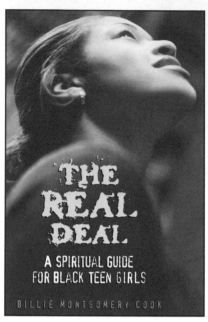